ONE CHURCH, ALL PEOPLE

BILL VICTOR

high street press

General editor: Brianna Boes

Cover design: Laura Schembre

Layout: Brianna Boes

Production management: Leah England

High Street Press is the publishing imprint of the Missouri Baptist Convention
(MBC) and exists because of the generous support of Missouri Baptists
through the Cooperative Program. To learn more about the MBC and the
way its 1,800 churches cooperate voluntarily for the sake of the gospel, visit
mobaptist.org.

CONTENTS

Introduction   v

Chapter One: Begin with the End in Mind   1
Chapter Two: "As it was in the Beginning…"   13
Chapter Three: The Diversity of the Early   29
Church and Conflict Resolution
Chapter Four: Destroying the Dividing Wall of   61
Hostility
Chapter Five: The Ministry of Reconciliation   73
Chapter Six: The Christ Hymn and   83
Reconciliation
Appendix   99

Notes   111
About the Author   125

INTRODUCTION

Two successive incidents occurred in my home state that brought a national spotlight to the problem of racial unrest. In 2014, a teenager named Michael Brown was killed by a Ferguson police officer. This event incited weeks of protests which provoked a strong police response as well as destruction of public and private property.[1] In 2015, years of unresolved reports of racial slurs and abuse directed at minorities on the campus of the University of Missouri came to a head. This led to a series of protests by Concerned Student 1950, a group particularly concerned with a lack of response from school officials. One student's hunger strike followed by a boycott of the football team gained national media attention. This eventually resulted in the resignation of the president of the university.[2]

These incidents caused many Missouri pastors to reflect and ask themselves how they could be part of the solution to rising racial tensions in our state (and nation). Many of us chose to ask people of color questions about the experience of being a minority in our society. This allowed us to see the perspective of our friends as they told us their stories.

These events prompted a multi-racial group of pastors and ministers to begin gathering in my city for breakfast once a month for fellowship and discussion. These were great times of learning about the differences and commonalities between us all. These discussions helped us empathize with each other and gave us a renewed sense of working together for the advancement of the gospel in our cities.

Unfortunately, these gatherings eventually faded away. Events alone rarely produce enough steam to promote real, long-lasting actions which result in healing among diverse groups in our communities.

The purpose of this study is to show that diversity and racial reconciliation are biblical issues; this is not just a holdover from the Social Gospel Movement. Diversity and reconciliation are seen in the Bible from beginning to end. When one examines Scripture with an eye for healing these tensions, perhaps a biblical mandate can be found, asking believers to work to heal the wounds of racial division.

This study hopes to give pastors, Bible study teachers, and interested lay leaders a practical guide that reveals how racial and cultural diversities reflect the heart of God. If fellow church members can be shown how this idea is found throughout Scripture, perhaps it can propel all believers to make these ideas a reality in their churches and in their communities.

Chapter One begins with a vision of the end — new creation (Rev. 21-22 NIV). This chapter surveys the diversity found in the new creation that is ushered in at the second coming of Christ. The Bible doesn't propose that all races and cultures will blend into one; rather, the biblical picture is one where worship in heaven reflects the diversity found on earth.

If diversity is included in God's plan for his people, then all Christians should be working toward this purpose here and now.

Chapter Two shows how this diversity was part of God's plan from the very beginning. Humanity was made in the image of God, and the mandate to "fill the earth" (Gen. 1:28) resulted in different cultures all reflecting the fullness of God's image in people.

Chapter Three looks at the book of Acts. The call to be witnesses in Samaria and "to the ends of the earth" would have confronted several of the early church members' prejudices. Samaritans and Gentiles lay outside their understanding of who could be a part of the people of God. Interacting with Samaritans and Gentiles would have exposed the early Christian Jews to charges of religious impurity. The early church also dealt with tensions that arose from within which stemmed from their own cultural diversity.

In Chapter Four, Paul writes to Gentiles who may have struggled with thoughts of unity with their Jewish brothers and sisters in Christ. Paul wants them to know Jesus has destroyed all racial and cultural barriers and has created a new people group in him.

In Chapter Five, Paul teaches the Church that each member of the Body of Christ represents the reality of new creation in advance. The ministry of reconciliation that God has given to all disciples of Jesus is not just working to reconcile people to God through their gospel witness. They are also called to work for reconciliation between all people.

Chapter Six shows how the beautiful Christ Hymn of Philippians 2 is more than just a great song extolling the incarnation and exaltation of Jesus. It is an ethical instruction for all believers to humble themselves and work for the betterment of others, just as Christ did. This chapter looks at how having the same sacrificial attitude of Christ can compel the work of healing racial and cultural tensions.

The Appendix looks at a few practical steps everyone can take as they seek to participate in the work of the reconciliation of all people.

A WORD ABOUT RACE IN THE BIBLE

The concept of racial reconciliation is anachronistic to biblical times because the concept of race was regarded differently in the biblical world than in modern times. Jarvis Williams surveys this well in his recent contribution to the book *Removing the Stain of Racism from the SBC*. In Deuteronomy 7:1-24, Moses defines Israel's racial identity in contrast to other nations based on geographical, theological, and ethical boundaries. These boundaries distinguished God's people from their neighbors.

In the New Testament, the word *genos* is used to distinguish people from other races, kinds, classes, or groups. Luke identifies Aquila as a Jew from the *genos* of Pontus. This suggests that geography contributed to one's racial identity from Luke's perspective (Acts 18:2). Both Jew and Pontus are categories that focus on different aspects of Aquila's racial identity. In a similar way, Luke identifies Apollos as a Jew from the *genos* of Alexandria (Acts 18:24). From Luke's perspective, Apollos' race was Jewish and Alexandrian. Peter calls Jewish and Gentile Christians a chosen *genos* as he applies language Moses used to refer to Israel (cf. Exod. 19:5-6; 1 Pet. 2:9).[3]

The Greek term *ethnos* (nation, Gentile) overlaps with *genos*. Both terms function as racial categories. The plural term "Gentiles" (*ethnikoi/ethne*) always refers to non-Jewish people and/or non-Jewish territories in the New Testament. The term *ethne* in the plural does not refer to people groups as much as it does to non-Jewish groups and/or non-Jewish territories (e.g. Matt. 6:32, 12:21; Acts 10:45, 11:1).[4]

Most of the racial and ethnic tensions in the Bible are related to the distinctions between Jews and Gentiles. Though biblical writers did not use modern racial and ethnic terms, it is still obvious that these differences caused tension. Resolving this tension was of particular interest to the writers of the New Testament.

DISCUSSION QUESTIONS

1. Name some people of color that you follow on social media. Have you read any minority pastors or thinkers for opinions on social issues?
2. If a "flash point" issue involving race arose that impacted your community, do you know any people of color with whom you could have a conversation?

CHAPTER ONE

BEGIN WITH THE END IN MIND

S tephen Covey's book, *The 7 Habits of Highly Effective People*, has sold over twenty-five million copies since its first publication in 1989. It has been hailed by *Time* magazine as one of the most influential business management books.[1] Covey's habits permeated American culture as concepts from the book reached even those who never read it. Phrases like "put first things first," "think win-win," and "sharpen the saw" have been quoted by many church and business leaders.

The suggested habit that captivates me most is to "begin with the end in mind," which means to start each day, task, or project with a clear vision of a desired direction and destination and then continue with a proactive mindset.[2] The idea is that the goals created in the mind prompt actual work. This habit is based on the ability to imagine intangible goals as if they were tangible objects. It's sort of like constructing a building. First, the architect envisions the creation. Then he or she creates a blueprint. Finally, the actual project can be constructed.

This concept applies to life goals as well. If you don't make a conscious effort to visualize who you are and what you want in life, you unwittingly empower other people and circumstances to shape you and your life by default.[3] A Christian's ultimate goal is recreation in the image of Christ. Envisioning the end goal — being like Christ — can inspire a spiritual formation plan to facilitate the process. Of course, Christians must rely on the Holy Spirit for every step.

NEW CREATION

All Christians have the personal goal of working toward Christlikeness. They can choose the spiritual disciplines that best suit them as they strive toward that goal, but there is also a corporate goal within Christendom. God gave humanity a glimpse of the end, a glimpse of the new creation.

End times should not be considered without including the new creation. Believers won't simply be transferred to some disembodied state in heaven. When the end comes, a new heaven and a new earth come with it.

The book of Revelation reveals a timeline of judgment before the great white throne. People will be judged according to what they have done. Anyone whose name is not written in the Book of Life will be thrown into the lake of fire. (Whether this is a literal lake of fire or a symbol of eternal separation isn't clear, but it isn't desirable either way.)

Revelation 21:1-5 gives further insight. The story of the Bible — the story of redemption throughout history — will end in a grand finale at the end times, but there's more to it. The renewal of God's whole creation will take place. God has worked all this time to return humanity to the restored and perfect creation as it was before the Fall, and this work will finally be complete.

A big part of the "good news" is that evil will ultimately be destroyed by God. God's wrath and judgment will fall on those who have not entered into a saving relationship with Jesus Christ, but for Christians, the "good news" does not end with judgment. Instead, they will experience a new heaven and a new earth where righteousness and peace dwell because God dwells there with his redeemed people from every nation.

Revelation 22:1-3 restores the language of Eden. John sees a river of water. On each side is the tree of life, bearing much fruit each month. Once again, just like Adam and Eve, humanity has access to the tree of life. The river flows from the throne of the Lamb, Jesus Christ, who gives life. The curse of the Fall is removed by his death on behalf of all people. God's ultimate purpose is realized as a new humanity lives with him in a new creation.[4]

Revelation 21-22 pictures life under the restored rule of God. It is life without threat, sin, pain, suffering, or death. It is a life of blessing, abundance, and security. It is a life of true freedom. The power of sin and death lies broken. Christians are free to be what they were intended to be — people who know and worship God. And that is good news.

Revelation 22:3 mentions that the leaves of the tree of life are for the healing of the nations. The idea of a diverse collection of people worshiping the Lamb and streaming into the New Jerusalem plays an important part of this vision of diversity in heaven. This chapter looks at three passages more closely in order to paint a picture of the diversity represented by those worshiping God in the new creation. This highlights the universal appeal of the kingdom movement that all Christians should be working toward.

THE PURPOSE OF REVELATION

What is the purpose of the book of Revelation? For the
Christians of John's generation, especially in Asia Minor
(southwest Turkey today), the exaltation of Rome and the
popularity of emperor worship made faithful Christian living
difficult and the future disturbing. Believers experienced great
pressure to join the majority in the celebration of Caesar's
divinity. Informers were eager to report to the authorities when
Christians refused to do so. Yet to yield to such pressure
entailed the denial of the Christian faith in its entirety, which
was unthinkable. John therefore wrote at the command of the
risen Lord to strengthen the faith and courage of believers, to
strengthen them for battle with anti-Christian forces, and to
help them bear witness to the one true Lord and Savior.[5]

The whole book of Revelation is rooted in its portrayal of
God Almighty as the Lord of history and its portrayal of his
redemptive activity in Christ. So surely as Jesus has
accomplished the first and most important stage in the
redemption of humanity, so he will complete his appointed
task of bringing victory to the kingdom of God and thereby
the total emancipation of humanity from the powers of evil.
The followers of the Lamb cannot expect to avoid sharing his
sufferings; hence the call early in the letters to the churches:
"Be faithful, even to the point of death, and I will give you life
as your victor's crown" (Rev. 2:10). That "victor's crown" is the
eternal company of God with the redeemed in the eternal city
of God.[6]

The reality of pagan Rome ruling the world and
oppressing Christians could have brought feelings of
powerlessness, frustration, envy, and a desire for vengeance to
those pledging allegiance to King Jesus as they awaited the
revelation of the fullness of God's kingdom. In short, this

situation could have distracted these first century Christians from pursuing Christlikeness. Instead, John gave them a vision of the universal scope of the praise of Jesus which included every tribe, tongue, people, and nation (Rev. 5:9-10; 7:9-10).

Revelation 5:9-10

And they sang a new song, saying: "You are worthy to take the scroll and to open its seals, because you were slain, and with your blood you purchased for God persons from *every tribe and language and people and nation*. You have made them to be a kingdom and priests to serve our God, and they will reign on the earth" (emphasis added).

The first few chapters of Revelation contain words of warning and encouragement to the churches in Asia Minor. John then receives a glimpse of worship in heaven. God is on his throne receiving worship from the heavenly beings as well as the twenty-four elders. God holds a scroll containing the judgments that are to befall the kingdoms of this world for their failure to recognize King Jesus and for their persecution of the people of God. Jesus, portrayed as a lamb who was slain, is the one worthy to open the scroll. The heavenly creatures and the twenty-four elders continue to worship the Lamb. By his blood, he purchased for God persons from *every tribe and language and people and nation*. The people from these nations are made to be a kingdom of priests to serve our God. This is a portrait of the universality of the sacrifice of Jesus.

These terms (tribe, language, people, nation) were meant to emphasize universality. The fact that Christians were drawn from many ethnic groups in the Roman Empire but did not constitute an ethnic group themselves led early Christian authors to refer to Christianity as a new people or a third race in contrast to Jews and Greeks.[7]

John records that those worshiping before the throne "sang a new song." This reflects the language of the many songs that Israel sang to celebrate God's redemption of his people (Ps. 33:3; 40:3; 96:1; 98:1; 144:9; 149:1). Psalms 113-118 especially focus on songs of praise commemorating deliverance from Egypt in the Passover and Exodus. Originally, the focus of that praise was to celebrate God choosing his people "from among all nations and tongues." As with ancient Israel, God has delivered his people, but the blood of the new Passover Lamb covers a people comprised of all nations and tongues.[8] In contrast to the exclusivism of Judaism, the Church was genuinely universal, recognizing no national, political, cultural, or racial boundaries.[9]

Those persecuted for their refusal to participate in the worship of the emperor may have been struck with the contrast of the illusion of human power. In various regions throughout the empire, regional choruses sang the emperor's praises. But an audience immersed in the Old Testament would be most struck by the fact that this new act of redemption encompassed believers from all peoples praising the Lamb on the throne instead.

Revelation was written to encourage suffering believers who were a minority in their communities in the first century. Just as the book of Daniel announced the rule of the Son of Man over all peoples, nations, and languages (Dan. 7:14), John sees a literal fulfillment of this promise in the Church.[10]

Who would benefit from such a book today in our own communities? Christians may find as they reach out to those who are suffering and those who live in the margins of society that these minorities can identify with a suffering Savior. Those Christians who find themselves in the minority may find special encouragement in this passage as Gentile believers probably did at the end of the first century. God's concern for all peoples may prove especially encouraging to groups that feel left out in their communities or in their church.[11]

Jesus redeemed for himself a people from among all nations and warns against the dangers of looking at ethnic identity as superior. Multiculturalism is not just a fad or an invention of theological liberals. God desired a multicultural Body of Christ from the very start (Matt. 28:19; Acts 1:8). Indeed, early Christians networked across the Mediterranean world. Apparently, Christianity was the only religion in the early Roman Empire that developed relations spanning many regions. This implies that God is impartial; he cares for all peoples. That acknowledgment in turn demands that his people love fellow believers across racial and cultural lines, which means there should be a willingness to hear diverse perspectives.[12]

Revelation 7:9-10

"After this I looked, and there before me was a great multitude that no one could count, from *every nation, tribe, people, and language*, standing before the throne and before the Lamb. They were wearing white robes and were holding palm branches in their hands. And they cried out in a loud voice: 'Salvation belongs to our God, who sits on the throne, and to the Lamb'" (emphasis added).

John sees that 144,000 were sealed from the tribes of Israel and spared from the wrath of the Lamb. Immediately after this, John notes that he saw a great multitude from every nation, tribe, people, and language standing in praise before the throne and the Lamb. These had come out of the great tribulation. The point here is not to distinguish a timeline but to note, again, the universal nature of the people of God.

The symbols of the white robes and palm branches are

symbols of victory. This multinational, multiethnic crowd has accessed the victory Christ won by his triumph on the cross. Christ did all the work here; none of these people inherently deserve these honors.[13]

That the multitude is countless is reminiscent of the promises to the patriarchs (Gen. 13:16; 15:5; 32:12). But here the promised multitude is gathered from all nations; the hope of the gospel has touched all peoples just as Jesus declared that it would (Matt. 24:14). It is striking that Christians appear here as a group "no one could count" since the number of Christians living toward the end of the first century would not have been very large. This vision would have encouraged John (and his readers) concerning the future success of the Christian mission.[14]

If the Church claims any loyalty to Christ's gospel, this requires members to transcend their cultural prejudices both to witness to unbelievers and to lovingly embrace believers from all cultures.[15] Christians cannot think that the gospel eliminates cultural distinctions. Likewise, it is unreasonable to expect Christians from other cultures to completely assimilate to American cultural norms when it comes to worship. This text (along with the others examined) suggests that, far from eliminating culture, God takes what is useful in each culture and transforms it into an instrument of praise for his glory.[16]

Revelation 21:24-26

"The nations will walk by its light, and the kings of the earth will bring their splendor into it. On no day will its gates ever be shut, for there will be no night there. *The glory and honor of the nations* will be brought into it" (emphasis added).

This passage in Revelation comes after Christ's thousand-year reign, Satan's defeat and banishment to the lake of fire, and the judgment before the great white throne. John sees a new heaven and a new earth, and then the new Jerusalem comes down from heaven. There is no need for the sun and moon because the glory of God and of the Lamb provide light.

John then writes that the nations will walk by its light and kings will bring their splendor, glory, and honor into the new Jerusalem. The reference to kings and nations in the new creation reveals that cultural and even national diversity is not abolished by redemption. Salvation does not erase cultural differences; rather, the human race, still distinguished by nationality, will walk by the glory or light of the holy city which will be illuminated by the Lamb (Rev. 21:24). According to this passage, "the unique contributions of each nation to the life of the present earth will enrich the life of the new earth. We will inherit the best products of culture and art which this earth has produced."[17]

The international character of God's people at the fulfillment of the biblical narrative brings to realization God's purpose from the beginning. God created all people, and Israel's election was for the sake of the nations (Gen. 12:1-3; Isa. 42:6-7). Such an understanding of the international character of God's people should lead the Church to actively seek to embody all that is good from the complex cultures of the world. Ethnocentrism is defined as judging other people groups by the standard of your own people group.[18] Ethnocentrism is not an option in the new creation.[19]

This passage in Revelation calls to mind Isaiah 2:1-5. Isaiah sees a day in the future, a future where the Lord's temple — the house of the Lord which was situated in Jerusalem on Mount Zion — becomes the most important place in all the world. The picture here is that the city is raised higher than all the mountains on earth. People are drawn to it, almost as if it has a magnetic pull, because that is where the Lord dwells. It is on this mountain that the people learn God's ways, not just to know them but to "walk in his paths." Their desire is to live according to his laws.

Not only does this place draw the nations, but the law goes out from this place. Instead of settling conflicts with warfare, the Lord resolves their disputes. The nations turn their weapons into farm equipment. This could also be what John sees as the "healing of the nations" in Revelation 22:3.

Isaiah 2:5 encourages, "Come, people of God. Let us walk in the light of the Lord!" This is the calling of all Christians. This is why God has chosen the Church. Believers represent a good God and draw the godless nations to his temple, ushering in an age of peace, wisdom, and true prosperity.

CONCLUSION

The international focus of Revelation is central to New Testament teaching. The thought that Gentiles could be grafted into God's people was radical. This is not surprising today; it is by far the norm. But perhaps modern believers can still learn from the principle that God embraces those whom they do not expect. This could help Christians witness to groups that are very different from them, such as Muslims, Hindus, and others against whom they might harbor suspicion.[20] The new creation will be filled with diverse nationalities, ethnic groups, and languages. This assured outcome should inform our mission.

The Church today already embodies a significant foretaste of the vision of diversity in Revelation. This vision anticipates the gathering of God's saints from "every tribe…" made into a new humanity and redeemed by Christ for the priestly task of reigning on this earth (Rev. 5:9-10). Not only are these multiethnic worshipers, but their earthly reign manifests the "salvation" for which they praise God. It is this comprehensive and holistic vision of God's kingdom that should guide the Church in reading Scripture and living in expectation of Christ's return. The overall thrust of the biblical canon (from creation to new creation) unveils a vision of the kingdom of God that is both applicable to every dimension of earthly life and open to the entire human family. Do not reduce the gospel of the kingdom to anything less.[21]

Remember the title of this chapter, "Begin with the End in Mind." It doesn't matter how Christians work toward unity; it is going to happen. As such, Christians should actively be part of the process.

Unlike a home project that goes unfinished or a hobby that never materializes into something useful, God's kingdom is a project on its way to meaningful completion. Its roots are in Genesis when God commanded humanity to "fill the earth" (Gen. 1:28), and it continued to grow in the New Testament when Jesus said, "Go and make disciples of all nations" (Matt. 28:19). It bears fruit in the spreading of the gospel today, and the glimpse of new creation given in Revelation should inspire Christians to expend their energy toward a common goal — bringing those of every tribe, tongue, people, and nation to the Lord Jesus Christ.

DISCUSSION QUESTIONS

1. How do you think we will display our ethnic and/or cultural distinctions in light of Revelation 21:24-26?
2. How could you view Christians of other cultures as allies in the midst of a society that is becoming

increasingly more hostile to evangelical Christianity?

3. As Christians become more marginalized in our nation, what can we learn from those who have had to live this existence already as Christian minorities?

4. Is it hard for you to separate your national identity from your Christian identity? In your mind, which comes first to you?

5. Does the "assured outcome" of human diversity in the new creation inform the mission of your church? If so, how?

CHAPTER TWO

"AS IT WAS IN THE BEGINNING..."

W hat is this universe, and how did humanity get here? Where did all this come from, and why does it exist? The answers to these questions can be found in Genesis 1, where the story of creation is recorded. It is especially compelling to look at Genesis through the lens of its original readers.

There were other creation stories in the Ancient Near East. One of these stories was the *Enuma Elish* which tells of a great war within the pantheon of gods that existed before the creation of the earth. This war resulted in one god vanquishing another and then fashioning the earth out of that god's carcass. Then, the victorious god created human beings out of another defeated god so they might serve as slaves to the gods. A picture of chaos, strife, and slavery is painted by the *Enuma Elish*.

Christians today can get bogged down in the specifics of the creation story in Genesis. The goal of this chapter is not to dig into whether there was a literal six-day creation versus the "age-day" theory, nor is it to tackle other attempts for modern readers to understand the science behind the Bible's creation story. Instead, the goal is to examine overarching themes of the Bible's creation story and how it provides a compelling counterpoint to other Ancient Near Eastern stories like the *Enuma Elish*.

In contrast to the *Enuma Elish*, the story of Genesis reveals no chaos or strife among the gods. It starts, "In the beginning, God…" There was no pantheon of gods struggling for control, but there was one God completely in control. God did not fashion the earth out of preexisting material but spoke the world into existence. God called all he had created good. Humans weren't created as slaves of God; they were created to fellowship with him and with each other.

Over and over in Genesis 1, God declares his creation good, and on that last day, after creating humanity, he called his creation *very* good.

IMAGE OF GOD

In the narrative of God's creation of humanity, it states:

> Then God said, "Let us make mankind in our image, in our likeness, so that they may rule over the fish in the sea and the birds in the sky, over the livestock and all the wild animals, and over all the creatures that move along the ground." So God created mankind in his own image, in the image of God he created them; male and female he created them. God blessed them and said to them, "Be fruitful and increase in number; fill the earth and subdue it. Rule over the fish of the sea and the birds in the sky and over every living creature that moves on the ground" (Gen. 1:26-28).

There is something different about the creation of humanity. Throughout the story, the narrative reads, "Let there be light… let there be a vault between the waters… let the land produce vegetation…" It almost seems impersonal, but when God creates the man and woman, he says, "Let us make mankind in our image, in our likeness…" There is something different about the creation of man and woman — an intimate involvement and personal investment.

What is the text saying by affirming that God created humanity, male and female, in his image? Right after creation, God gave humans a commission: "Be fruitful and increase in number; fill the earth and subdue it. Rule over the fish in the sea and the birds in the sky and over every living creature that moves on the ground" (Gen. 1:28).

Already the difference is clear between the Bible's creation story and others from the Ancient Near East. In the *Enuma Elish*, humans were created as slaves to meet the needs of the gods. In the Bible, God created humanity in his image to be guardians over creation. He assigned them a task and provided the means to accomplish that task. God tailored creation to the needs of humans, not to his own needs (because he has no needs). God sought relationship with humanity and set them up to rule over his creation.

In the Ancient Near East, the notion of the "image of god" was often reserved for rulers, the kings and pharaohs of the land. Kings were regarded as special servants of the gods and bore their image as rulers of the earth. In this passage, perhaps God is saying that *humanity as a whole* shares in God's rule over the earth. Instead of being reserved for just a privileged few, it extends to everyone. All humanity is created in the image of God. This shows that God is a generous creator who shares authority with the height of his creation.

Kings and emperors in the ancient world (and even a few

dictators in our modern world) would set up images of themselves throughout their territory. These great statues proclaimed the king's authority over that territory and its people. Similarly, God installs humans as his image within creation and authorizes them to exercise authority. But that authority ultimately belongs to God, the creator and owner of the earth.[1] So, if human beings are meant to function as "kings" or "rulers" within creation who represent God on earth, then the people of God need to know what kind of king God is. How does God exercise his kingship within creation?

Psalm 145 is one place to turn. This psalm is addressed to "my God the King" who is characterized by wisdom, power, goodness, grace, compassion, faithfulness, generosity, provision, protection, justice, and love. If that's what it means for God to act as king, then the same qualities should be seen in the way God's people, who are made in his image, exercise the dominion that God has entrusted to them.

One of the primary responsibilities of the kings of the Old Testament was to act on behalf of the weak and powerless. In Psalm 72, David implores God to endow the king with justice so he can defend the afflicted and needy and rescue them from oppression and violence.[2]

God's commission to humanity to rule over creation includes the calling to act as the image of God the king. This means believers are to work toward good stewardship in relation to the rest of creation. It means that the mission of God's people — to care for creation — is inherited from the mandate given to the first couple.

There is so much to learn about God and about oneself by understanding the creation of humanity in the image of God. Going beyond the notion of humanity as simply good caretakers of God's creation brings a deeper, richer understanding.

One facet of the image of God is personality, which can be seen in humanity through interpersonal interactions. People think, reflect, and act with some degree of free will. Humanity was intended to know, love, and obey God. People were also created to live in harmony with each other and experience deep relationships.

Being made in God's image makes every person valuable. The sacredness of human life is an extremely important principle in God's plans. Even after the Fall, murder was prohibited based on the fact that people are created in the image of God (Gen. 9:6). The implication is that even after the Fall, humanity did not lose the image of God. There is something wrong with humanity's relationship with God; it is no longer unbroken as it was in the Garden. However, humans still retain something of the image of God. People can only experience the fullness of humanity when living in an unbroken relationship with God.[3]

The image of God in humanity is universal. It is found in both men and women. It extends to all races and ethnicities. There is a dignity to being human. Even after the Fall, there remains the potential for all humans to be conformed to the image of the Creator. It follows that believers must be careful in how they relate to others. Hatred and abuse reveal a lack of care and devotion to God and a lack of understanding when it comes to humanity's original purpose — to relate properly to God and to each other.

FILL THE EARTH

The first twelve chapters of Genesis show that God created people in his image (Gen. 1:26-27; 5:1; 9:6). He blesses them and gives them the command to fill the earth (Gen. 1:28; 9:1; implied in 9:7). Genesis 10:32 reveals that, from the sons of Noah, all nations spread out over the earth after the flood.

Humanity spreading out over the earth was not mere coincidence. The idea was first reflected in the plan of God at creation. The first human beings were directed to fill the earth and bring it under their dominion. To achieve this, people needed to procreate and multiply in number, and as they populated the earth, they needed to spread across it.

As the migration after the flood took place, these wanderers encountered different types of environmental conditions, and as they adapted to their surroundings, different cultural lifestyles emerged.[4] For instance, new and previously unknown weather patterns would have required adaptation regarding things like clothing and building construction. As humans moved to regions where they were exposed to different intensities of sunlight, the result was a diversity of skin color. Variations in human skin color are adaptive traits that correlate closely with geography and the sun's ultraviolet radiation.[5]

God's command to fill the earth resulted in different people groups. The development of different cultures didn't take God by surprise (nor was it the result of the Fall). This is what God had intended from the beginning. Cultural differences and diversity were always part of God's original plan. When God commanded the first humans to "fill the earth," it was a decree to create cultures because no one culture, people, or language can adequately reflect the splendor of God.[6]

Genesis 10 is known as the "Table of Nations." The language of this chapter expresses the idea that all humanity is descended from a single stock. All men are sons of Noah as well as sons of Adam.[7] The world is one united family, all of whom can trace their origin back to Noah, who in turn owed his existence to the saving act of God.

Although Hebrews were the specially chosen agents of divine revelation, they were but one member of the universal family of nations.[8] Genesis 10 emphasizes Israel's commonality with other nations more than it does their uniqueness. What the chapter affirms is that all humanity, in spite of geographic and linguistic differences, shares a common origin founded in humanity's nobility and inherent value.[9]

The Tower of Babel episode in Genesis 11 seems out of place in light of the notion that chapter ten is stressing the commonality of all nations. God has to spread the people out himself because their common language has enabled them to settle and work together to set themselves up against God. This is not a contradiction of the theme of Genesis 10:32 but rather a reaction to the fact that humanity disobeyed the original command of God. God wasn't intimidated by this refusal to carry out his original intent for humanity. He confused their language, which forced them to scatter and brought about the fulfillment of his original purpose for humanity.[10]

To view culture and ethnicity as simply consequences of sin obscures God's larger purposes and distorts the role of diversity in human relationships. By putting chapter ten before the Tower of Babel episode, Scripture removes the negative stigma from diversity. Thus, the dispersal of humanity reflects God's blessing.[11]

"... ALL PEOPLES ON EARTH WILL BE BLESSED THROUGH YOU ..."

In the chapter after the Tower of Babel episode, God begins his plan to redeem all individuals and nations who have rebelled against him. After Noah gets drunk and passes out naked in his tent, he curses his son Ham for revealing his nakedness. He also blesses his son Shem who acted honorably toward him. In spite of this curse, hope remains for the descendants of Ham. It is from the descendants of Shem that all peoples on earth will be blessed (including the line of Ham) through the family of Abraham.

The creation account shows God blessing his creation. Blessing could be characterized by fruitfulness, abundance, and fullness, or it could be described as enjoying rest in an unbroken relationship with the Creator. The blessing God bestows on Abraham, his family, and all the peoples of the earth includes these concepts of fruitfulness, multiplication, spreading, and abundance. It is a richly life-affirming promise. God wants these blessings for the nations of humanity, and he desires each person to experience them in full.[12]

The major idea behind the promise to Abraham was that "all people on earth will be blessed through" him. This promise is repeated five times in Genesis (18:18; 22:18; 26:4; 28:14). There is a universal end in view. If humanity as a whole is subject to God's curse (because of the disobedience of Adam and Eve), then humanity as a whole must be reached through God's blessing.[13]

God addressed one man, Abraham, and promised to bring his blessing to humanity through one nation, Abraham's descendants. One nation was chosen, but all nations were to be beneficiaries. Eventually, one nation would be represented by one man, Jesus, through whom God's redemptive blessing would become available to all nations. As seen in Galatians 3, Paul understood God's mission through Christ to be the spreading of the gospel as the fulfillment of God's promise to Abraham.[14]

The promise to Abraham of blessing for the nations is Paul's mandate for mission.[15] It is also foundational to Paul's understanding of salvation. Christians are saved by faith without needing the signs of Jewish identity because God's plan was always for his blessing to extend beyond the nation of Israel.[16]

Abraham became the father of many nations (Gen. 17:5) because he is the father of the faithful. He became the pattern of salvation for all nations (not just the ethnic sons and daughters of Israel). Through Abraham, Scripture teaches that a right relationship with God comes through God's grace and our faith in his promises. That right relationship is the beginning of the restoration of the relationship God originally planned for the first man and woman.

After bringing the family of Abraham out of Egypt, God made an agreement with them. He promised to be their God and called on them to obey him. God told them, "… out of all nations you will be my treasured possession." God called Israel to be a priestly kingdom in the midst of all nations (Exod. 19:4-6). Israel as a whole was to take the knowledge of God to the nations and bring the nations to the means of atonement with God. Holy means "set apart." To be a holy nation was to be a distinctive nation. They were to reflect the holiness of God and make him known to the other nations.[17]

Along with making God known, the Israelites were to welcome people from other nations. "You are to love those who are aliens, for you yourselves were aliens in Egypt" (Deut. 10:19). The prophets reveal that God planned something new for Israel; he would encompass all nations within his chosen people (Isa. 11:10-16; 19:18-25). "Many nations will be joined with the Lord in that day and will become my people" (Zech. 2:11).[18]

God called out this people, formed them from the family of Abraham, and made them his own. His purpose in this was for them to be a "light for the nations" (Isa. 49:6). Israel was to model what a people blessed by God looked like. He made a promise and gave them his word in which they could trust and abide. In Deuteronomy 4:5-6, Moses tells the people:

> I have taught you decrees and laws as the Lord my God commanded me, so that you may follow them in the land you are entering to take possession of it. Observe them carefully, for this will show your wisdom and understanding to the nations, who will hear about all these decrees and say, "Surely this great nation is a wise and understanding people."

Israel was to model life under the rule of God through obedience to his word. In this way, the nations would see that God's rule brings life and blessing. They would see what it was like to know God and have him near. Israel commended God and his kingdom to the nations.[19]

In the grand story of the Bible, humanity goes from being the "clans, languages, and nations" of Genesis 10, who stood in confusion and in need of redemption, to that "great multitude that no one could count, from every nation, tribe, people, and language" who make up the redeemed community in the new creation (Rev. 7:9). This is the real beginning of the good news in the light of Genesis 3-11: God has committed himself to bless all the people of the earth.[20]

In general, the purpose of Genesis 10 (Table of Nations) is to show the continuation of the blessing. People continue to be fruitful and multiply, but they are also filling the earth. Beyond these basics, however, the Table of Nations offers a specific picture of the world. The point is that all the known nations and peoples resulted from the blessing God had established from the beginning. National and ethnic diversity were not aberrations. There is no room for the concept that there is one pure race while others are tainted, somehow the result of sin or corruption.[21]

IMAGE OF GOD, IMAGE OF CHRIST

What does it mean for humanity to be made in the image of God? What is God's intention for humanity within this life and creation? The answer lies in believers patterning their lives after Jesus who is the complete revelation of the image of God. He is the full image of God, and he is the one person whose humanity was never spoiled by sin. According to F. F. Bruce, "To say that Christ is the image of God is to say that in him the nature and being of God have been perfectly revealed — that in him the invisible has become visible."[22]

What God intended for Adam, Jesus accomplished. The role of the first man and woman was to rule over creation. Now the perfect representation of God has come. Jesus achieved his status as ruler over creation through his obedience to the Father, something the original pair did not accomplish. Jesus enabled humans to have a right relationship with God, of which their disobedience had deprived them. Only Jesus, who is the perfect image of God, can rescue the distorted images of creation.

The character and actions of Jesus are helpful guides in the discussion of what it means to be created in the image of God. He is the perfect example of what human nature was intended to be. First, Jesus has perfect fellowship with the

Father. While on earth, he communed with and frequently spoke to the Father. This is best evident in John 17. Second, Jesus obeyed the Father's will perfectly. In the Garden of Gethsemane, Jesus prayed, "Father if you are willing... but not my will, but yours be done" (Luke 22:42). He said elsewhere, "I seek not my own will but the will of him who sent me" (John 5:30). In accordance with God's will, Jesus always displayed a strong love for people. He had great patience with and forgiveness for those who failed him (John 21:15-23). He had compassion for the sick (Mark 1:41), and he had a deep concern for the lost sheep of Israel (Matt. 9:36; 10:6). It is God's intention that a similar sense of fellowship, obedience, and love should characterize the believer's relationship to God and that they also be bound together with one another in love. People only experience the fullness of what it means to be human when displaying these characteristics.[23]

Part of the salvation process is that the image of God is gradually restored. Believers are being conformed to the Jesus-version of that image (Rom. 8:29). Deliverance brings about a gradual transformation into the glorious humanity of the Lord Jesus Christ (2 Cor. 3:18; 4:4). In that renewed image, Christians become immortal rather than mortal, heavenly rather than earthly (1 Cor. 15:49). In the new creation, headed up by the new Adam (Jesus), the new humanity reflects the original image of its Creator (Col. 3:10). When believers are seated with Christ, they are returned to their proper human state (Eph. 2:6; Col. 3:1; Rev. 20:4). As already discussed, God made human beings to rule with him and to rule for him. This return to humanity's dominion in the new creation begins for those who trust in Jesus in the present.[24]

James 3:9-10 states: "With the tongue we praise our Lord and Father, and with it we curse human beings, who have been made in God's likeness... this should not be." The implication is that all persons bear the "likeness" of God and have a special dignity. People should not curse other people because they are made in "the likeness of God."[25] This idea has significance for this study and in contemporary relations within modern communities.

One way God's image brings dignity to humanity is found in the unity of mankind. This unity is evident whether one goes back to Adam or only as far back as Noah. It is clearly revealed that God "made from one every nation of men" (Acts 17:26). There are many indications of the universality of the gospel in embracing people of all nations (Matt. 28:19; Acts 15:7; Rev. 5:9), and in every case, the basis of acceptance is the same. The New Testament speaks of no conditions which apply to one race and not another and gives absolutely no sanction to any theory of racial superiority.[26] All men and women of every tribe, language, people, and nation have dignity and value because they have all been created in the image of God. Those who are rightly related to God and are being remade to reflect that image more sharply should lead the way in pursuing unity within the diverse images of God in their communities and in their world.

This belief in human dignity affects the believer's view of how society responds to human needs, such as sickness, imprisonment, bereavement, poverty, or defenselessness. Christians can and should seek to shape the society around them in ways that preserve human dignity. When rights are granted grudgingly or coerced through demands, dignity is lost from the equation. If Christians truly believe in the dignity of all, rights and their protection must follow automatically. But preservation of dignity is not an inevitable result of protection of rights. Christians should go farther. If minority groups are treated with dignity, they won't wonder whether they were given a job only because of rights issues. If women are treated with dignity in the workplace, they will not suffer degrading harassment.[27]

God's design for humanity was to represent him and fill the earth with his image. While diversity is not a result of the Fall, the lack of harmony between people groups is. The goal of God's blessing of Abraham's family was for his people to pursue God's original design for his creation. God's people are to take his image, now more clearly defined as the image of Christ, throughout the earth to bless all people and bring them back to a sense of reconciliation and common origin. This leaves no room for racial strife or ethnic division.

DISCUSSION QUESTIONS

1. Genesis possibly locates the Garden of Eden in what is modern-day Iraq. Does that help you picture the ethnic identity of Adam and Eve? When you picture the first couple created in the image of God, how do you picture them ethnically? Does the fact that so much of the biblical narrative takes place in what today is known as the Middle East help inform how you picture the features of the main characters?

2. Why do you think humanity is so ethnically and culturally diverse? How does God's commission to "fill the earth" play a part in our diversity?

3. Deuteronomy 10:19 reads: "And you are to love those who are foreigners, for you yourselves were foreigners in Egypt." How does this inform your attitude toward immigrants and asylum

seekers? How should the Great Commission impact our views on immigration?

4. In this chapter we learned that diversity is not a result of the Fall; the lack of harmony between people groups is. What is your church, small group, etc., doing to promote racial harmony? How should it motivate us to think that our disunity is a sign of the Fall?

CHAPTER THREE

THE DIVERSITY OF THE EARLY CHURCH AND
CONFLICT RESOLUTION

A cts of the Apostles is a valuable document for the Church as it links the records of Jesus to the apostolic correspondence. In many ways, the epistles are not fully intelligible until they are read against the background of the book of Acts. The book shows the development of Christianity and presents the continuing work of Jesus through the apostles. It makes a valuable contribution to the discussion of the relationship between the teachings of Jesus and the doctrines of the apostles. It is the only extant historical account of the early church outside of the epistles.[1]

There are many proposals about the purpose of Acts. Acts has been seen as a defense of the Christian Church to Rome, an apology for Paul against the Judaizers, and a tool of the Church's evangelistic mission. All agree that Acts was written to deepen the faith of new believers like Theophilus.[2]

This chapter will not debate the purpose behind Luke's writing of Acts. Instead, the focus is on reading Acts in light of the struggle for racial reconciliation. There are several episodes in Acts describing tension between people groups and how the early church resolved this tension. While the problems facing contemporary society do not exactly mirror the racial and cultural tensions in Acts, there are still some things to learn about conflict between people groups which can be applied to situations today.

THE ACTS 1:8 CHALLENGE

Acts 1:8 has been called the table of contents of the book of Acts. When the apostles asked Jesus if he would restore the kingdom to Israel, he responded: "But you will receive power when the Holy Spirit comes on you; and you will be my witnesses in Jerusalem, and all Judea and Samaria, and to the ends of the earth." The apostles were still focused on a desire to see the enemies of Israel vanquished and Jesus the Messiah ruling from a throne on Mount Zion. Jesus instead outlined a mission which empowered the apostles through God's Spirit to spread the gospel throughout the world. This mission didn't end with Rome as the ends of the earth. It extended to all peoples, everywhere. Paul saw the challenge to bring salvation to the ends of the earth as equal to God's desire for his people to be a light to the Gentiles (Acts 13:47; cf. Isa. 49:6). By using Paul's language here, Luke gave evidence that the challenge to be Jesus' witnesses to the ends of the earth is a mission to all peoples — Jews, Samaritans, and Gentiles.[3]

How would this mission sound to Jews who still longed for the restoration of the kingdom of Israel? The answer comes with an examination of the attitude of native-born Jews toward Samaritans and Gentiles, which shows how great the challenge was to these apostles and how they would have to overcome the stigma attached to non-Jews.

"My Witnesses in... Samaria"

Most everyone who has attended Sunday School is familiar with Jesus' parable of the good Samaritan. The parable has such impact because of the tension between the original Jewish hearers and their Samaritan neighbors. A little background may prove helpful.

Jesus himself was a victim of the tension between these groups. Luke recorded that as Jesus "resolutely set out for Jerusalem," the Samaritan village he planned on passing through did not welcome him because of where he was going (Luke 9.51-53). In John's Gospel, when Jesus asked a Samaritan woman for a drink, the woman replied, "How can you ask me for a drink?" John adds an interpretive comment, "For the Jews do not associate with Samaritans." From this context comes the parable of the good Samaritan; it shocked the Jews because the Samaritan in the story is the ideal neighbor.

Who were these Samaritans, and how did this animosity arise? The root of the tension between the Jews and the Samaritans originated with the division of the kingdom of Israel. Samaria was the capital of the northern kingdom. In 722 BC, the Assyrians invaded the northern kingdom, captured Samaria, and deported thousands of Israelites to areas throughout the Assyrian kingdom. The king of Assyria brought people from other conquered areas to settle in the northern kingdom and replace the Israelites. These new people did not worship the God of Israel. Eventually, an Assyrian king sent Jewish priests, who had previously been exiled, back to live in Samaria to teach the people how to worship the Lord. But the imported groups continued to worship their own gods, going so far as to sacrifice children.

Thus, these returned Israelites worshiped the Lord but also the gods of foreign nations.[4]

After the southern kingdom of Judah experienced its own judgment and exile, many of those in exile were allowed to return to their homeland and rebuild the temple in Jerusalem. Samaritans offered to help rebuild the temple, but the leaders of the building project rejected their offer. This began a series of false claims of rebellion against the people of Jerusalem from Samaritan officials to their Persian overlords. This extended to the time of Nehemiah's project of rebuilding the wall around Jerusalem.

There were other political tensions between the groups. Jews resented Samaritans for their acceptance of the Greek culture and worldview. Plus, the Samaritans refused to join the Maccabean rebellion against Antiochus Epiphanes. Later, one Jewish ruler captured Shechem and destroyed the Samaritan temple on Mount Gerizim. Then some Samaritans scattered bones in the Jerusalem temple during Passover around AD 6 or 7.[5] In the rabbinic writings, one of the ancient rabbis said: "He that eats the bread of the Samaritans is like one that eats the flesh of swine."[6] This verse is found in the Apocryphal book of Sirach: "Two nations my soul detests, and the third is not even a people: Those who live in Seir, and the Philistines, and the foolish people that live in Shechem [the capital of Samaria]."[7]

Jesus' command for the apostles to be his witnesses in Samaria was counter cultural and could have been seen as repugnant had the apostles not been filled with the Holy Spirit. The call to go to the ends of the earth and bear witness to the Gentiles would have been seen as even more objectionable.

"... to the Ends of the Earth."

How awkward this must have sounded to native-born Jewish ears. Samaria served as a bridge between the Jewish world and that of the Gentiles. While Jews had conflict with Samaritans, their difficulties with Gentiles were even more pronounced (specifically for Judean Jews, like the apostles).

Most of the aversion to socializing with Gentiles came from the holiness laws of Judaism. There was a real concern about what impact regular relations with Gentiles would have on purity and personal holiness.[8] As Christian Jews became more open to taking the gospel to Gentiles, it remained a point of conflict with non-Christian Jews. While Christianity grew committed to encountering the world in its universal mission to convert it, Judaism remained committed to keeping its people pure and unstained by the unclean (Gentile) world.[9]

God's covenant with Abraham created the nation of Israel. God set Israel apart from other nations as his chosen people (Deut. 7:6-8), and he gave them a land to possess (Gen. 15:8) and the Law to obey (Exod. 19:3-6). Thus, being a Hebrew was a matter of ethnicity, politics, and religion. The word "Gentile" referred to anyone falling outside of these delineations (e.g. Deut. 15:6; 2 Sam. 7:23; Ps. 115:2-8). The prevailing Jewish attitudes toward Gentiles saw them as unrighteous (Deut. 18.9; Gal. 2:15) with no hope for salvation (Eph. 2:12).[10]

The New Testament gives evidence of some justified Jewish attitudes toward Gentiles. Jesus criticized Gentiles for their manner of praying (Matt. 6:7). He also referred to Gentiles as sinners who greet only their friends (Matt. 5:47), who pursue material things (Matt. 6:32), who think God answers long-winded prayers (Matt. 6:7), and who use power to their own advantage (Mark 10:42).[11] Jesus told his followers to treat unrepentant members of the community "like a Gentile or tax collector" (Matt. 18:17).

Paul criticized the sexual immorality of Gentiles (1 Cor. 5:1; 1 Thess. 4:5). Paul connected their worship of idols to worship of demons (1 Cor. 10:20) and regarded their sinfulness as a sign of spiritual ignorance (Eph. 4:17). Peter listed "debauchery, lust, drunkenness, orgies, carousing, and detestable idolatry" as typical Gentile behavior (1 Pet. 4:3).[12]

The practice of avoiding certain kinds of contact with Gentiles preserved Jewish identity. Jews held the fundamental conviction that since Israel had been chosen by God, they were required to keep separate from other nations to maintain holiness before the Lord.[13] These restrictions were displayed the most during fellowship at meals, which was the main expression of hospitality or friendship and the principal occasion for the transmission of impurity (Acts 11:3; Luke 7:34).[14]

There was some integration with Gentiles (especially in the Diaspora). For instance, Gentiles were allowed in the synagogues, and there were business transactions between Jews and Gentiles. But there were areas of life in which Jews were resistant to Gentile ways. Jews were intent on separation from Gentiles and paganism because of Gentile sinfulness. They prohibited Gentile participation in temple worship and exhorted Jews not to marry Gentiles. The Jews revolted violently when Gentiles tried to impose religious reforms on them, and they believed Gentiles would one day be judged and punished by God.[15]

In spite of all this, a persistent feature of Judaism was a positive attitude toward a true proselyte who abandoned paganism to become a Jew, both spiritually and nationally. There was also the expectation of massive conversion of Gentiles on the Last Day. This conversion was frequently portrayed in terms of Gentiles flocking to Zion instead of Jewish missionaries reaching out to Gentiles (Isa. 19:23; Zech. 8:21; Jer. 3:17). Even though there was reference of proselytism by Jesus (Matt. 23:15), this really wasn't a common practice within Judaism.[16]

Though Gentiles were in dire straits spiritually, there was hope for them in the gospels. Jesus wanted the gospel preached to the nations, which implied Gentile inclusion in the kingdom of God (Matt. 22:1-14; 24:14; 25:31-46; Mark 13:10; Luke 11:29-32; John 10:16). This leads to Jesus' command to take the gospel to the ends of the earth. Jesus challenged his apostles to be witnesses among all people, not just those like them.

DIVERSITY AT PENTECOST

Jesus told the apostles to wait in Jerusalem for the Holy Spirit to come upon them to empower them to be his witnesses in that city, in all Judea and Samaria, and to the ends of the earth. Ten days afterward, the Holy Spirit came to rest on those who were waiting. They were filled with the Spirit and began to speak in other tongues. This was a momentous occasion for this small band of Jesus followers, and it ushered in a new age in the history of salvation. The Holy Spirit would no longer rest upon men and women for an occasion or to fulfill a task but would dwell within believers to empower them for his mission.

Readers can get caught up in a discussion about the "tongues" in which the apostles spoke. Was it *glossolalia* as Paul describes in 1 Corinthians 12-14 or other known languages which the Spirit enabled these believers to speak? That is a discussion for another time. For this study, it is more important to look at the catalogue of nations and people groups present in Jerusalem at Pentecost.

Pentecost (meaning fifty) is the Greek term for the Jewish festival called the Feast of Weeks (see Lev. 23:21; also known as the Feast of the First Fruits). It was called Pentecost because it was to be celebrated seven full weeks after the Sabbath following Passover.

Jews throughout the world came to the Jerusalem temple for the special sacrificial offering to take place on that day (Num. 28:26ff.). Pentecost was the second of three great annual festivals of the Jews, with Passover and the Feast of Tabernacles being the others. The greatest number of pilgrims attended the Feast of Pentecost because at that time of year the weather was more conducive to travel.[17] For many Jews, this festival was a celebration not simply of the offering of the first fruits of the wheat harvest but of the renewal of the covenant made by God with Israel at Sinai.[18]

In Acts 2:5, Luke mentions there were "God-fearing Jews from every nation under heaven" staying in Jerusalem at this time. There were definitely Jews who had moved back to Jerusalem after living abroad, but it is probably Luke's intent to call attention to the great many pilgrims visiting specifically for the festival.[19] The Church's proclamation of the mighty works of God begins with faithful Jews. But when Luke calls attention to the pilgrims "from every nation under heaven," he foreshadows the universality of the mission. From the very first day, the good news of Jesus' resurrection was heard by a wide range of Jews.[20]

In Acts 1:9-11, Luke provides a "catalogue of nations" of Jewish pilgrims who hear the apostles speak in "other languages." This catalogue includes fifteen ethnic groups or regions in which these Jewish pilgrims lived.[21] The list includes the following: Parthia (modern Iran), Mesopotamia (modern regions in the Middle East), Judea (modern Palestine and perhaps Syria), and Cappadocia, Pontus, Asia, Phrygia, and Pamphylia (all of which are part of modern Turkey). Luke even mentions Jews from North Africa, Rome, Crete, and Arabia. Jewish pilgrims had come to Jerusalem from three continents and from over fifteen hundred miles away![22]

The effectiveness of spreading the good news to so many pilgrims can be seen when Paul arrives in Rome to a Christian community already established in the city (Acts 28:15). The reference to Rome in Acts 2:11 could be a hint by Luke that the Christian community there originated with the Jews of Rome who visited Jerusalem during the Feast of Pentecost. It is likely that these Roman Jews heard the message of Jesus the crucified and risen Messiah, were converted to faith in Jesus, and took the good news of Jesus back to Rome.[23]

The worldwide scope of the Christian witness is anticipated at Pentecost with this list of nations. Though these people of different lands were ethnically (or at least, religiously) the same, they were culturally very different. As these pilgrims went back to their regions with the gospel, they would have also crossed racial barriers. Thus, the gospel was shared with "every nation (*ethnos*) under heaven."

Pentecost foreshadowed the worldwide mission. This passage is an extension of the idea that the gospel should be taken "to the ends of the earth."[24]

DIVERSITY AND CONFLICT — ACTS 6:1-6

So many today have an idyllic picture of the early church. The portraits in Acts 2:42-47 and 4:32-35 reveal a church that met together on a regular basis, praising God and devoting themselves to the teaching of the apostles. They had devotion to one another, and they lived with glad and sincere hearts.

They went to great lengths to meet each other's needs. They "were one in heart and mind." But another, less perfect picture is portrayed in chapters five and six. There is the deceit of Ananias and Sapphira (Acts 5:1-10) and the conflict between the "Hellenists" and "Hebrews" (Acts 6:1-6).

Luke uses the story of the conflict between the "Hellenists" and "Hebrews" to point the early church toward a mission beyond Jerusalem. He directs them to the next phase where Acts 1:8 is lived out.[25] Luke then gives attention to the work of those outside the Twelve, especially Stephen and Philip.[26]

Acts 6:1 presents the juxtaposition of two realities in the new community: a growth in the number of disciples and a management problem that this growth produced among the Hellenists and later the Gentiles.[27] This episode also introduces a pattern for resolving congregational conflict, which is repeated throughout the Church's mission.[28]

This book takes interest in the cultural and ethnic issues the early church had to work through. Though a community open to all peoples lends itself to tricky situations, the early church found a way to navigate these potentially destructive situations.[29]

The Plight of the Widow

At the heart of this episode, a certain group of widows was being neglected in terms of food distribution. This was a serious problem for a group grounded in the Hebrew Scriptures, which provided injunctions for God's people to care for the most vulnerable members among them: widows, orphans, immigrants, and the poor and powerless (cf. Lev. 19, 25; Deut. 16:11; Mal. 3:5; 1 Tim. 5:3-16; James 1:22-2:17). The prophets made it clear that the treatment of these members effectively gauged Israel's relationship with God.[30]

It wasn't just that widows in general were being neglected. Hellenistic Jewish widows were specifically being left out. This passage reveals that the united body of believers was made up of at least two contrasting groups: Hellenists and Hebrews. The word "Hellenist" means one who uses the Greek language.[31] In the same vein, the word "Hebrew" here in context means "one who speaks Hebrew or Aramaic."[32]

There would have been many Greek speakers among the native residents of Jerusalem. So what is the source of this tension that Luke describes in chapter six? The Hellenists here were more than likely Jews from the Diaspora who came to settle in Jerusalem. Their language and their lifestyle tended to be Greek in nature. They may not have spoken Aramaic. They even had their own synagogues (Acts 6:9). As so happens with ethnic groups, they tended to associate with those who shared their language and cultural background.

As the Church increased, some of these Hellenists became Christians. It is only natural that these Greek-speaking Jewish Christians would have formed close associations with one another, perhaps even meeting in home fellowships together.[33] This situation is not unique and happens even today. It is entirely understandable that a monolingual community would group together for communal activities in a city where the language of everyday life was unfamiliar to them.[34]

This isolation could have led to tension between the Jews who moved to Jerusalem from the Greek-speaking world and the Aramaic-speaking natives. For Jews living in and around Jerusalem, speaking Aramaic and living a thoroughly Jewish lifestyle were tied to a nationalistic identity with Israel. This would have aroused a suspicion of anything that looked foreign. This tension could have gone both ways. The Hellenists more than likely looked down on the Hebrews as narrow-minded and more traditional. Equally, the Hebrews probably regarded the Hellenists as those who were diluting and compromising key traditions of their shared faith and practice.

These Hellenistic widows may have moved with their husbands later in life to be closer to the temple and to be buried in the land of Israel. As the men died, they left behind widows who were far away from family members who could help take care of them. That left those women vulnerable and in need of provision. The community as a whole took it upon themselves to care for these widows. Contemporary Judaism made provisions for the needy, like these widows. A weekly stipend for the resident needy was given out every Friday and consisted of enough money for fourteen meals. Food and drink were distributed daily to needy nonresidents and travelers as well.[35]

This care for the needy was passed on to the early Christian community. Originally, the administration of the community charity seems to have been in the hands of the apostles (Acts 4:35). But old suspicions surfaced in the church between natives and immigrants. Immigrant widows were being neglected in the distribution of food for the needy. An "us versus them" mentality took root as resentment divided these two distinct groups.[36] Even though both groups were committed to the same Messiah, they lived separate lives, socially and perhaps even geographically (within their own enclaves inside of Jerusalem).

This was more than just the growing pains of numeric growth. This situation reflects underlying tension between these two factions.[37] As people contributed to the treasury of the church in order for the apostles to make sure no one needed anything, the Hellenistic widows were being overlooked in favor of the Hebrew widows because the distribution of provisions was in the hands of Hebrew

Christians. This may have been mere oversight, but the perception was that the neglect was based in old animosities between the Greek-speaking Jews and the Aramaic natives.

The Solution

The early church recognized this conflict needed to be resolved. Neglect because of prejudice cannot be maintained and supported in a community that confesses a Messiah who has come to give God's grace to all people.[38]

The first step in resolving internal conflict is to bring together all those involved and include them in creating the solution. This episode with the neglect of widows indicates that the church should be a cohesive congregation whose regular experience is serving God together with "one heart and mind." There is the presumption of solidarity — of shared faith and abiding friendship — that provides the basis for this meeting of the disciples.[39]

The Twelve recognized it was important to meet the spiritual and physical needs of this community. The apostles were inheritors of the teachings of Jesus, and it was important for them to preserve these teachings and expound on them. One of the applications of Jesus' teaching was to love one's neighbor as oneself. That meant these physical needs had to be addressed. As the church grew, the apostles couldn't be devoted to both the ministry of the Word and overseeing the distribution of funds for the needy, though it was extremely important.

The Twelve gathered all the disciples together (or most likely, representatives of all the disciples). Though the Hellenists presented the complaint, the problem involved the entire congregation.[40] As leaders of the community, the apostles proposed that the members choose seven men from among them to administer the charity to the Hellenist widows. The context suggests that the seven men chosen were also Hellenist. These men would know better who the needy widows were and how to communicate with them.

The apostles affirmed the congregational decision by laying their hands on those chosen seven. This gesture is used to commission someone or a group to a task (see also Acts 13:3). While the oversight of such a commissioning speaks to the authority of the apostles, it also says something about the seven. They were given authority directly from the apostles. One use of the laying on of hands was for commissioning a successor (Num. 27:23). In this instance, the laying on of hands by the apostles formally associated the seven with the Twelve as their deputies to discharge a special duty.[41] By selecting these seven, the apostles were then free to carry out their primary responsibilities of preaching and bearing witness of Christ.[42]

This unit shows the community using its own people to solve its own problems. The community heard the complaint, owned up to the problem, allowed those closest to it to solve it, delegated the authority to get it done, and then went to work. The issue was not denied or papered over but confronted directly as a community concern.[43]

Lessons for the Church

The early church displays several important features in this passage.

First, there is continuity with Judaism in showing concern for those in need. This episode suggests that a community's compassion is measured by how it cares for the poor, the orphaned, and the widowed. This speaks to the community's character and credibility as a place where concern is met with action.[44]

Second, the fact they were able to come up with so many Hellenist leaders points to the early church's multiethnic and multicultural roots. The adopted solution also reveals that the disciples did not fragment along cultural lines nor did they condone the church doing so. They were committed to working together.[45] Unity was maintained because the church worked to take care of the physical needs of a neglected group.

James D.G. Dunn, a British theologian and scholar, makes an interesting observation. He notes that the way Luke presents this episode reveals he may have used Hellenist sources. Luke himself acknowledges that he used sources to compile his work (Luke 1:1-4). This suggests that this episode is an account provided from a Hellenist perspective.[46] If this is true, Luke allowed the minority culture to tell its own story instead of filtering this account through the lens of the majority culture.

Luke and the other Gospel writers did not avoid mentioning embarrassing incidents in the life of the early church, such as the tension derived from the clash of cultures and worldviews. They stayed true to the reality that a shared faith among diverse groups produces diverse ways of practicing that faith. Suspicions and resentments arose which led to factions and even schism.[47] Still, the early church did not shy away from diversity. In fact, diversity in language, culture, and socio-economic status was present at the start. Christianity has always known the tensions which come from diversity of culture and viewpoint.[48] When the early church faced these clashes of culture, they met the problem head on and gave the Church an example of how to seek unity.

After this issue was resolved, the next few chapters of Acts show the Church reaching beyond itself. Not only were Stephen and Philip equipped to take care of the needs of the Hellenist widows, they were equipped for other forms of service as well. Stephen defended the faith in the Greek synagogues in and around Jerusalem and before the Sanhedrin. Philip was equipped for the work of evangelism among the Samaritans.[49] The mention of Nicolas has special significance as well. He was the first Gentile mentioned in Acts who decided to follow Jesus. Plus, he was a native of Antioch, which foreshadows the work to the Gentiles Luke later recorded in Acts 11:19-30.

PHILIP'S MISSION IN ACTS 8

Chapter eight of Acts continues to build the bridge between the predominantly Hebraic Jewish Christian church in Jerusalem and the mission to the Gentiles foreshadowed by the conversion of Paul in chapter nine. In chapter eight, two new classes of people previously held at arm's length (at best) from Judaism are welcomed into the Church of Jesus Christ, that is, Samaritans and eunuchs.

Philip's mission yielded some surprising converts to Christianity. Both the Samaritans and the Ethiopian eunuch were seen as marginal Jews, removed from Israel's promised blessings. The Samaritans were considered religious renegades as well as racially impure by more traditional Jews. While the eunuch may have been seen as a "pious pilgrim," his physical condition disqualified him from becoming a proselyte to Judaism.[50]

Philip in Samaria

From a Jewish perspective, Samaritans were neither Jew

nor Gentile but rather their own category. Descended from the northern tribes of Israel, they still considered themselves the people of God. Samaritans had their own form of the Pentateuch for their holy scriptures. They circumcised their sons and built a temple on Mount Gerizim to rival the one in Jerusalem. They continued to worship God in their own independent manner and to look for the "*taheb*," a prophet-like messiah who would restore true worship on Mount Gerizim. This was a messianic expectation based on Deuteronomy 18:15. To the Jews, the Samaritans were half-breeds and heretics. They were also seen as politically untrustworthy because the Roman occupation of Palestine was headquartered in Samaritan Caesarea.

Philip's mission into Samaria was a radical step toward Stephen's vision of a gospel free of nationalistic prejudices.[51] John's story of Jesus' journey through Samaria is introduced by the phrase, "Jesus had to go through Samaria..."[52] The geographical necessity of Jesus' detour foresees its theological necessity. Jesus went through Samaria as part of God's redemptive plan. In continuity with Jesus, this account of Philip's Samaritan mission is governed by divine purposes.[53]

The Samaritans had the same misgivings about the Jews. This wasn't a one-way street. These tensions give the success of Philip's mission that much more meaning. As the Samaritans observed the display of the Holy Spirit through Philip, they paid close attention to his message and received it with great joy (Acts 8:8).

Many Samaritans (along with Simon the magician) believed the gospel and were baptized. But they did not receive the Holy Spirit until Peter and John laid hands on them in prayer. There has been much debate about the delay between the water baptism of the Samaritans and their reception of the Holy Spirit. Is this a text giving evidence of a second blessing? No. The pattern of repentance, baptism, and reception of the Holy Spirit is revealed in Acts 2:38: "Repent and be baptized, every one of you, in the name of Jesus Christ for the forgiveness of your sins. And you will receive the gift of the Holy Spirit." But there are a few incidents in Acts where the actions of newly baptized believers gave visual evidence of the reception of the Holy Spirit. This only happened when the Holy Spirit came to a new region or a distinct group received the gospel for the first time. This is evident with the Samaritans here, the Gentiles in Acts 10, and John the Baptist's disciples in Ephesus in Acts 19. It is not a universal experience.

Why, then, is there a delay between the acceptance of the gospel, baptism, and the receipt of the Holy Spirit with the Samaritans? Why did the apostles need to lay hands on them? The reason for the delay may have been to make it clear to the apostles that God had acted. They could now give visible witness to the phenomenon. Normally the Spirit came with faith, but these were special circumstances which warranted a break in the pattern in order to underscore a fresh move of God. The inclusion of the Samaritans was filled with potential controversy. The presence of Peter and John may have been designed to help the Jerusalem church accept what was happening in a land that was not considered a beneficiary of grace.[54] This is similar to the episode in Acts 6. Through the apostles' laying on of hands, they conferred a status of acceptance on a group of people and legitimized their mission efforts.

The Samaritan mission was given a stamp of approval from the church in Jerusalem. It was not just the undertaking of a maverick Greek missionary. It was endorsed, received, and enthusiastically participated in by the whole church.[55] The text goes on to say that Peter and John continued to share the gospel in Samaritan villages on their way back to Jerusalem. Just as there had been the healing of a rift between the Hellenists and the Hebrews in Acts 6, there is a healing of centuries-old tension between Jews and Samaritans — all done in the name of Jesus Christ. The gospel has tremendous power to bring together groups that not only held one another in suspicion but actively despised one another.

The Ethiopian Eunuch

There are several questions about how to classify the Ethiopian eunuch. Is he a Gentile and therefore the first Gentile convert in the book of Acts? Or is he more closely aligned with Judaism similar to a proselyte? This section shows he could not have been seen as a full proselyte to Judaism, but Luke does not portray him strictly as a God-fearing Gentile. Luke seems to shape his narrative to represent Cornelius and his household as the first Gentile converts.

In the ancient world, slaves were often castrated as boys in order to be used as keepers of the harem and the treasury. Eunuchs were found to be particularly trustworthy and loyal.[56] This Ethiopian man's physical condition prevented him from being a full convert to Judaism (Deut. 23:1). He seems to be caught between proselyte and Gentile. Luke portrays him as someone tied to Judaism beyond a deep respect for Israel's God (like many God-fearers). This is a man returning from a pilgrimage to the temple in Jerusalem (where he was forbidden from entering the temple for worship). He owns and is studying a scroll of the prophet Isaiah. Darrell Bock, professor of New Testament studies at Dallas Theological Seminary, places the eunuch in a category similar to a Diaspora Jew, a man who would have become a proselyte if he was physically capable of going all the way. He would not be classified as a Gentile in the manner of Cornelius.[57]

Ben Witherington, an American biblical scholar, argues that the ancient world regarded Ethiopia as "the end of the earth," so the gospel reaching Ethiopia was the fulfillment of the announcement in Acts 1:8. The gospel not only reached the end of the earth but also included those in the margins of and those excluded from Judaism.[58]

The book of Isaiah mentions Ethiopia's participation in the blessings of God (Isa. 18:1; 45:15). God promises in Isaiah 56:3-8 to give eunuchs and foreigners who hold fast to the covenant and who keep the Sabbath a place in his temple. It is likely that this passage in Isaiah was of special significance to the eunuch. This Ethiopian eunuch who traveled to Jerusalem to worship represents both of these excluded, disowned groups as the recipients of God's promise.[59]

The passage the eunuch read (Isa. 53:7-8) may have resonated with him. Visiting the temple but being denied entry, despite his devotion and piety, may have humiliated him. The figure in the passage in Isaiah was despised and rejected. The eunuch may have felt rejected, since he could not fully experience worship at the temple. The eunuch was also faced with a lack of descendants. Yet the rejected and despised figure in Isaiah would "see his offspring" after his suffering. He may have wanted to know of whom the prophet Isaiah spoke because the eunuch related to the figure mentioned in the passage.

As Philip used this theologically rich passage about the Suffering Servant to explain to him the good news about Jesus, the eunuch was convinced and asked, "What can stand in the way of my being baptized?" (Acts 8:36). The way this was written indicates all barriers were removed from his reception of the gospel. In this case, the barriers of both physical and racial prejudice had fallen. A Gentile man who was also a eunuch was baptized into full membership of the Church.[60]

It is interesting to note that the first converted Christian "foreigner" in Acts was an African. The gospel expanded to a new ethnic group, and one could say that the mission to Africa began long before Paul ever took it to Europe.[61]

The Church Becomes More Diverse

Acts 8 shows the expansion of the mission of God and how God worked mightily through a wide array of people.[62] The words of God to the prophet Isaiah were fulfilled in Philip's mission. Isaiah 56 foretold that God would one day gather the entire household of Israel — including both "foreigners" and "eunuchs" — for worship in celebration of God's faithfulness to his people. While Philip's mission in Samaria and his witness to the eunuch do not initiate the Church's mission beyond Israel, they are climactic episodes of Israel's restoration that began with Jesus' mission to Israel. These episodes also prepare the reader for the Lord's shocking commission of another Jewish convert who carries the word of God beyond Israel as "a light to the nations" (Acts 9:15).[63]

PETER AND CORNELIUS

Chapter ten marks a high point in the Church's expanding mission. God led Peter to witness to the Gentile Cornelius. Through that experience, Peter was fully convinced of God's purposes to reach all peoples. He became one of the greatest advocates of the mission to the Gentiles (even though he would need to be reminded of this; see Gal. 2:11-14).[64] A key feature of this episode is that witnessing to the Gentiles was not planned by the apostles or other members of the Church.

Rather, it was directed by God from beginning to end. It was God who sent the angel to Cornelius, directing him to send messengers to bring Peter to him. It was God who caused Peter to have the vision of the clean and unclean animals. It was God who told Peter to "not call anything impure that God has made clean," and it was God who poured out the Holy Spirit on the Gentiles without any prior action by Peter or the believers with him (like the laying on of hands).

Peter bringing the gospel to Cornelius is a truly groundbreaking event in the history of the mission of God. The Samaritans at least had circumcision and the Torah in common with the Jewish people. The Ethiopian eunuch gave signs that he would have been a full convert to Judaism if he would have been able to be circumcised. But in chapter ten, the Church is confronted with the question of Gentile membership in the people of God now reconstituted in Christ. This was a completely new concept. Outsiders had always been welcome to join God's people, but they were required to become Jews first. That included circumcision for male converts and adherence to the Torah. Converts to Judaism were expected to obey the food laws and carefully avoid becoming unclean according to the Law.

That the early church would have to struggle with whether Gentiles should be included in the Church without becoming Jews first is understandable. Jesus was Jewish and came first to the Jewish people. The apostles and all the early church were Jewish. The whole redemption movement had worked through Israel. When Gentiles wanted to become part of this movement, it was only logical that they become Jews. Now, God had to teach his people that those barriers had been destroyed. His household was now open to Gentiles with no restrictions outside of allegiance to Jesus Christ.

Cornelius' Vision

Cornelius was a Roman centurion stationed in Caesarea. He and his family are described by Luke as "devout and God-fearing." The term "God-fearer" was used later to describe Gentiles who adhered to Jewish law but had not become full proselytes to Judaism.[65] At the very least, Luke writes that Cornelius gave generously to those in need and prayed regularly. These are two of the three main acts of Jewish piety (the other being fasting).

Cornelius received a vision of an angel of God telling him to send for Peter. The next day, the Lord sent a vision to Peter to prepare him to receive Cornelius' messengers.

Peter's Vision

God's command to Peter to "get up… kill and eat" without regard for the cleanliness of the animals would have been regarded as unacceptable for a devout Jew. The Torah had strict regulations on what kind of food was clean or unclean. Eating the wrong type of meat could make a Jewish person ceremonially unclean, which meant they would have been excluded from the community (see Lev. 11; Deut. 14).

By the first century, these food restrictions took on a new emphasis. Not only was it a sign of being acceptable in God's eyes and in the community, it was a cultural sign distinguishing Jews from Gentiles. The heroes and heroines of Israel's history demonstrated their loyalty to their people and their God by refusing to eat the food of Gentiles. Peter is portrayed as thoroughly loyal to the ancestral traditions of the Jews of the time.[66]

In Mark's Gospel, Peter heard Jesus teach about what makes a person clean or unclean (Mark 7:1-23; Matt. 15:1-20).

One implication of this teaching was that Jesus had declared all foods clean (Mark 7:19). These words must have echoed in Peter's head as he received the vision and the command to kill and eat animals that were ceremonially unclean (Acts 10:9-16). Peter would have realized that Jesus' teaching and this vision had a greater meaning than just what foods he could eat.

God is preparing Peter through this vision for a new understanding of who belongs in the household of God. The character of the Christian movement as a Jewish movement was at stake. What did it mean to become a Christian? Did one need to remain loyal to the traditionally distinctive features of the covenant people? To be a Christian, was it necessary to adhere to the principles and practices for which Jewish martyrs had died, for which Jewish heroes and heroines had sacrificed everything? Before this incident, the answer would have been yes![67]

The messengers from Cornelius arrived as Peter pondered what God was trying to tell him by asking him to eat impure animals. The fact that Peter accepted the Gentile visitors and invited them to stay in his house until they could make the trip to Caesarea was a sign that God was breaking down Peter's resistance to his previous understanding of what was clean or unclean.

Peter Enters the Gentile's Home

Conscientious Jewish people like Peter were not only worried about what food they ate. They were also concerned with whom they shared a meal. The idea was that since Gentiles were careless with regard to food, they would also be careless in how they prepared their food. Even if a Gentile attempted to serve a kosher meal to a Jewish visitor, there were no guarantees the food would have been uncontaminated during its preparation. One can imagine the dilemma Peter faced as he approached Cornelius' home and crossed the threshold. For Peter to enter a Gentile home would have made him unclean regardless of whether he ate with them. The rabbis would later write: "The dwelling places of Gentiles are unclean."[68]

Peter was in the process of breaching a fundamental guiding principle of Jewish relationships and communal living: that Jews should keep themselves from Gentiles. This was not so cut and dried, since Jews living amongst Gentiles would have experienced public interaction. However, table fellowship was off limits. The conviction was that Israel as a nation had been chosen by God and therefore was required to keep itself separate from other nations to maintain its holiness before the Lord (Lev. 20:24-26). The primary testing point was the meal table, the main expression of hospitality or friendship and the principal occasion for the transmission of impurity.[69]

But Luke writes that Peter entered the house with no apprehension. Peter fully understood the vision God gave him. He mentions that even the Gentiles knew it was against Jewish law to visit a Gentile, but God had shown him he should not call anyone impure or unclean (Acts 10:28). As the law of clean and unclean had served to embody and defend Israel's separateness, so its abolition meant that the time of Israel's holding itself separate from the nations was over. If no animal was by nature unclean, then neither could any human being be designated that way. Peter was now free to deal with Cornelius as he would have dealt with any fellow Jew.[70]

The breakdown of ethnic and religious boundaries around Israel was indispensable and integral to the breakthrough of the gospel to the nations at large. The success of God's plan to bless all peoples of the earth (Gen. 12:3; Acts 3:25) involved a redefinition of Israel's own identity as it had previously been defined by separation from Gentiles.[71]

As Peter began his sermon, he said: "I now realize how true it is that God does not show favoritism but accepts from every nation the one who fears him and does what is right" (Acts 10:34-35). Peter echoed words from Deuteronomy 10:17-18 concerning God's impartiality. In its original context, God states that he does not show partiality among his people. He cares for all, including widows, orphans, and even foreigners. This impartiality is fully extended to Gentiles. To the impartial God, what makes a person acceptable is not a matter of ethnic heritage or nationality but reverence of God and doing what is right. Peter acknowledged that a person who fears God is as acceptable to God as the Jew, and that such a person is not required to submit to the legal requirements of the Torah. The God-fearing Gentile is as ready to receive the blessing which comes through the name of Jesus and the Spirit of God as the God-fearing Jew. The point is that Cornelius and his household were acceptable to God even as Gentiles, and full acceptance into the messianic Jewish community depended only on believing in Christ and receiving the Holy Spirit, as Gentiles instead of converts to Judaism.[72]

In Peter's message, Jesus is described as "Lord of all" (Acts 10:36). This title presents the theme of the speech. Jesus is exalted and is Lord over all people. Since he is Lord of all, the gospel can go to all, including people of the nations like Cornelius and his household. Jesus has the authority to deliver the peace that comes from God to those of every nation.[73]

The Gentile Pentecost

As Peter spoke, the Holy Spirit came on all who heard the message without any request from Peter or the laying on of hands as had happened with the Samaritans. God initiated this movement based on the faith of those hearing the gospel.

Luke fashions this outpouring of the Holy Spirit in the same manner as the original outpouring of the Holy Spirit upon the apostles on the day of Pentecost in Acts 2. First, when Luke writes, "The Holy Spirit came on all who heard the message" (Acts 10:44), he reflects Acts 2:4 which says, "All of them were filled with the Holy Spirit." Second, the circumcised believers were astonished at this outpouring of the Spirit (Acts 10:45), just as the bystanders in Jerusalem were "utterly amazed" at the outpouring of the Holy Spirit upon the apostles (Acts 2:7). Both groups began to speak in tongues praising the work of God (Acts 2:4, 11-12; Acts 10:46). Third, Peter mentions baptism as the next step for Cornelius' household (Acts 10:47-48), just as Peter had commanded in Acts 2 for the new believers to "repent and be baptized" (Acts 2:38). What happened to Cornelius and his companions was no different from what had happened to the first disciples on the day of Pentecost. How could Jewish believers witnessing this affirm one and deny the other? They could not.[74]

Peter asks in verse forty-seven, "Surely no one can stand in the way of their being baptized with water?" This is very similar to the question of the Ethiopian eunuch. Nothing could stand in the way of these Gentiles being baptized, not even the fact that they had not fully converted to Judaism. This incident proves that repentant Gentiles share the same gift of the Holy Spirit with repentant Jews. Peter says, "They have received the Holy Spirit just as we have" (Acts 10:47).[75]

Peter stayed with Cornelius for several days after this event. He now viewed these Gentiles as "clean." As there was nothing to hinder their being baptized, there was nothing to hinder their acceptance into fellowship. God directed this radical event. Their faith led to the gift of the Holy Spirit, the sign that the age to come had arrived (Acts 2:17; Joel 2:28-32). In addition, they were not circumcised, yet table fellowship and full hospitality between Jews and Gentiles ensued (here at least).[76]

The Objection by "The Circumcised"

News of this momentous occasion spread from Caesarea to Jerusalem. It might be expected that this event would have been met with great praise and rejoicing. The Gentiles were coming to faith in Christ. God was truly doing something new and exciting! God had promised Israel would be a blessing to all the peoples of the earth, and that promise was being fulfilled through Jesus Christ. But that is not how the news was received. Luke notes that the initial reaction was criticism toward Peter and his colleagues for visiting the home of a Gentile and eating with them.

God's work is met with criticism from a group Luke identifies as "the circumcised believers." It is hard to say who exactly this group is. Luke could be referring to the leaders in Jerusalem as a whole. However, since all of them would have been circumcised, why would he feel the need to make that distinction? Luke may be pointing to a group which felt very strongly that Gentiles needed to become Jews in order to be accepted into the people of God. This distinction may also be foreshadowing conflict that arises throughout the Greco-Roman world as Paul's mission to the Gentiles gains acceptance (Acts 15:1). In any event, the account in Acts 11 shows that the inclusion of Gentiles in the Church did not go without objection or debate.[77]

Just as Peter needed a vision from God and his companions needed to see God's work by witnessing the outpouring of the Holy Spirit, so the rest of the Jewish believers needed evidence to secure their acceptance of Gentiles into God's family.

The purpose of chapter ten was to allow Peter to tell his story and give witness to what he preached and what he saw — from his vision to the Roman centurion to the event where the Holy Spirit fell upon the Gentiles. For both Jew and Gentile, this reception of the Holy Spirit was promised by John the Baptist as the ministry of Jesus. How could Peter stand in God's way?

The complaints of the objecting group were silenced by Peter's story. They glorified God for his initiative in giving the Gentiles repentance that leads to life. They saw that God brought this about, not Peter. The circumcised believers (in Jerusalem at least) joined Peter and the others in seeing that God brings various ethnic groups into one in Christ.

Peter later refers to Cornelius' conversion and reception of the Holy Spirit as the model for the conversion of uncircumcised Gentiles and their solidarity with Jewish believers (Acts 15:7-11). Peter concludes his remarks at the council at Jerusalem by saying, "We [Jews] believe it is through the grace of our Lord Jesus that we are saved, just as they [Gentiles] are" (Acts 15:11).

This message is important in Acts: Jesus brings reconciliation not only with God but between people. The community of believers is diverse in makeup, equal in status, and called to reflect peace with one another. Peter is the example of one who understands and actively pursues this fresh opportunity. Indeed, he defends it here (and later, see Acts 15:7-11) as the will of God. God has opened a new way to himself for all people through Jesus.[78]

This reconciliation worked itself out in Peter's day with cultural sensitivity. Gentiles were not forced to become Jews. They were allowed to keep their ethnic and cultural identities alongside their new identity in Christ. As seen previously, diversity is part of God's plan. This approach reflected a respect for cultural roots that did not seek to make everyone in the Church exactly the same in unessential matters. Today, such issues surface when the gospel enters a new culture. In cross-cultural ministry, practices that are Western (or American) but not specifically Christian should not be imposed on others, and vice versa.[79]

CONCLUSION

These stories in Acts show that the work of ethnic and cultural reconciliation is not easy. Those who witnessed the teaching and resurrection of Jesus had to overcome prejudice. But, prompted by the Spirit of God, they worked toward reconciliation with all people at great cost and with great zeal, convinced their actions were done within God's will.

DISCUSSION QUESTIONS

1. Even though Hebrew and Hellenist groups both were committed to the same messiah, they lived separate lives. Is this true in your community? Are there like-minded believers with whom you have no interaction due to cultural differences? How could churches work together to rectify this? From whom within our biblical faith have we allowed ourselves to become separated?

2. In Acts 6, the apostles worked to make sure the diverse people in the early church were treated equally in the distribution of food. Are there groups in your community that are not being

treated equally that your church could work to help? Who are some people that you can think of that may be similar to the Hellenistic Jewish Christian widows in your community? How can your church help?

3. The eunuch was denied full entrance into Judaism because of his physical status. He may have felt despised and rejected. Who are those who feel despised and rejected in your communities that need the healing touch of the gospel? Are there those who do not feel like full participants in our churches because of their physical status (like those with disabilities)?

4. Are there certain behaviors (like the example of circumcision in Acts) we expect outsiders to exhibit before they are fully embraced in our church? Are there expectations on behaviors that keep us from seeing God at work among certain people?

5. Peter initially received criticism for the gospel work he did among the Gentiles. If you reached out to work with a group that was considered "impure" or unworthy, how would your church respond?

CHAPTER FOUR

DESTROYING THE DIVIDING WALL OF
HOSTILITY

The Jewish historian Josephus described a five-foot-tall partition in the temple of Jerusalem. This barrier was made of stone, and its purpose was to mark off the Court of the Gentiles from the Court of the Israelites. This barrier bore inscriptions warning Gentiles to keep out of the inner courts under punishment of death.[1] This was the only issue in which the Romans allowed the Jews to maintain the death penalty. Paul knew very well the seriousness of this offense. Acts 21:27-36 contains the story of the uproar caused when Paul was falsely accused of bringing a Gentile (Trophimus from Ephesus) into the temple. In Ephesians 2, Paul may be referring to this barrier as he describes the "dividing wall of hostility" that separated the Jews and Gentiles. In this chapter, Paul reminds these two groups that, in Christ, they are one new identity instead of two factions.

THE PURPOSE OF EPHESIANS

From the beginning, it was God's plan for his people to be holy and blameless in his sight (Eph. 1:4). In Christ, all things were created (Col. 1:16). This implies that at one time, after creation, the cosmos and humanity had an unbroken relationship with God. This is displayed in the first two chapters of Genesis. At the end of the creation story in Genesis 1, God declared everything he had made as "very good." Genesis 2 shows that God's people were placed in a garden full of beauty and provision. The first humans had a relationship with God that was not tainted by sin. But this status didn't last long. The very next chapter of the narrative reveals the man and woman losing faith in God's promises. They gave into temptation, and all humanity and creation suffered after that selfish decision.

God did not abandon his plan for a holy and blameless people. He chose Abraham and his family to become a source of blessing for all peoples. The family of Abraham became the nation of Israel. Their commission remained the same: to become a source of blessing for all peoples of the earth. Somehow, this status of being God's people became something to be protected instead of shared. God's law and his rules for holiness and purity were used to keep people separated from Israel instead of being seen as guidelines for the nations.

Paul reveals in Ephesians 1 that God's plan was to bring unity to all things in heaven and on earth (Eph. 1:10), returning creation to its original state. He accomplished this through Jesus Christ. Unity continues to be a key theme throughout the book of Ephesians, which was written mainly to Gentiles perhaps because of animosity directed from believing Gentiles to believing Jews.

The period from the Fall until the redemptive work of

Christ was filled with strife between nations, races, and religious affiliations. But now, Christ is the head of the whole Church (Eph. 1:22-23), including both believing Jews and Gentiles. Because believers have such a new and lofty status in Christ, Paul wanted his brothers and sisters to reflect on this status and how it relates to the unity of all people.

By reconciling all people to himself through the cross, Christ created a new humanity, marked by peace rather than hostility; this is displayed in the Church where Jews and Gentiles alike have access to God and compose what is now God's spiritual dwelling place (Eph. 2:11-22). This new unity of humanity is "the mystery of Christ" revealed to Paul when he was commissioned by God. Now, the Church's role is to make the mystery known, not only to the world of unbelievers but also to spiritual powers in heavenly places (Eph. 3:1-13).[2]

Paul uses the term "mystery" six times in Ephesians, always with the reference to something divine. The Greek term has a different connotation than the English understanding. It refers to something hidden that can only be known if revealed by someone possessing inside information. A divine mystery can be revealed only by God (Eph. 3:5), though in this case God has commissioned Paul and other "holy apostles and prophets" to disclose this mystery to the Church.[3]

This mystery concerns God's plan to unite all things in Christ (Eph. 1:9-10), specifically his plan to unite all *people* in Christ. This was God's intention all along, "hidden for ages" (Eph. 3:9) but coming to fruition "when the times reach[ed] their fulfillment" (Eph. 1:10). Ephesians 2:11-22 shows how the unity of humanity in Christ is evidence to the rulers and authorities in the heavenly realms that God's plan is being accomplished in Christ Jesus (Eph. 3:9-11).

A WORD TO THE GENTILES ABOUT RECONCILIATION — EPHESIANS 2:11-13

Paul begins this passage by asking the Gentiles to reflect upon their status before being accepted by God. This suggests Ephesians was written to Gentile converts who came into the church after Paul left Ephesus. It also suggests they were dismissive of the church's spiritual heritage and Jewish roots.[4] Just as there had been reservations by Jewish Christians toward full acceptance of Gentiles, there may have been Gentile reservations toward Jews based on generations of tension.

At one time, Gentiles were separate from Christ and excluded from citizenship. They were foreigners, without hope and without God. Paul may be trying to produce an attitude of profound thankfulness and a mindset that accepts the ethical implications of being a new, holy community — implications later addressed in the second half of the letter.[5] Despite such desperate circumstances prior to their reception of the gospel, Paul gives two glorious words of relief to these Gentile Christians: "But now... those who were far away have been brought near" (Eph. 2:13). The privileges now enjoyed by Gentile believers would be appreciated all the more if they bore in mind the state of life from which they had been delivered.[6] Prior to the work of Christ, Gentiles could only access the benefits of belonging to the people of God by becoming Jews.

Dividing Wall of Hostility

In verse fourteen, Paul tells his readers that Jesus is their peace. Not only has Jesus made peace (Eph. 2:14) and preached peace (Eph. 2:17), he is himself their peace. Jesus not only reconciled his people to God through his death, but he reconciled Jews and Gentiles. It is in him that his people enjoy this double blessing of peace. Jesus brought the formerly hostile groups into a new unity in which the old distinctions between Jew and Gentile were transcended.

The hostility between the two groups is well documented. In verse fourteen, Paul mentions "the barrier, the dividing wall of hostility." Paul may be making a reference to the dividing wall in the temple that separated the Court of the Gentiles from the inner sanctuaries to which only Jews could be admitted.

However, the dividing wall in the temple was probably not his only meaning. Paul mentions in the next verse that Christ's atoning work on the cross set aside the law with its commands and regulations. The law itself was a barrier alienating Gentiles. In later rabbinic teachings, the law was seen as providing "a fence around Israel." *The Epistle of Aristeas* declared:

> ... our lawgiver... fenced us round with impregnable ramparts and walls of iron, that we might not mingle at all with any of the other nations, but remain pure in body and soul... lest we should be corrupted by any abomination, or our lives be perverted by evil communications, he hedged us round on all sides by rules of purity, affecting alike what we eat, or drink, or touch, or hear, or see.[7]

In functioning as a fence to protect Israel from the impurity of Gentiles, the law became a sign of Jewish particularism that alienated Gentiles and became a cause of hostility.[8]

Laws which forbade eating with or marrying Gentiles often led the Jews to have a contempt for Gentiles, regarding them as less than human. In response, Gentiles would often regard

Jews with great suspicion — considering them inhospitable and hateful to non-Jews — and indulge in anti-Jewish prejudice. The Roman historian Tacitus wrote about the anti-Jewish sentiment among the elite of the Roman Empire:

> The Jews are extremely loyal toward one another, and always ready to show compassion, but toward every other people they feel only hate and enmity. They sit apart at meals, and they sleep apart, and although as a race, they are prone to lust, they abstain from intercourse with foreign women; yet among themselves nothing is unlawful.[9]

The "dividing wall" Paul mentions here invokes the image of the actual wall in the Jerusalem temple. The Jewish law that Christ abolished served as a metaphorical dividing wall because it defined the terms of a covenant that only applied to Israel. For the Jews, the cross of Christ creates a new way to be human, a way that does not privilege one national or ethnic group above another.[10] This would have been challenging for God's "treasured possession out of all nations" (Exod. 19:5).

Christ's abolishment of the law works toward the goal of unity. Jesus created a new humanity out of these two people groups. In this context, the one new person stands for the new humanity symbolized as the Church, the Body of Christ. Christ embraced this new person in himself. Paul argued that divisions of race and religion were a thing of the past (Gal. 3:28; Col. 3:11). Now, Ephesians reveals that Christ has taken the two divisive elements — Jews and Gentiles — and created one new person which transcends them both. This is a new creation which embodies, on a human level, the summing up of all things in unity.[11] It's easy to focus on the work God does in removing the barriers between himself and humanity, but the work of Christ shows that God is also concerned with removing barriers between all people and people groups. While Jews formerly spoke of the division of humanity into Jews and Gentiles, Paul created a third category: the Church of God (1 Cor. 10:32). No wonder the early church referred to themselves as a "third race" or "new race," no longer Jewish, no longer Gentile.[12]

Christ came to preach peace. It was obvious the Gentiles, "who were far away" from God (Eph. 2:13), needed to hear the message of peace. But Christ also came to preach peace to those who were near, that is the Jews. Both groups stood in need of peace with God and in need of peace with each other. Paul was unable to imagine a peace given by God to those far and near which would not also be a peace between the two. Peace is not simply a matter of the soul or of individuals only; if it is peace from God and peace with God, then it is also peace among people. By changing human social relations, God changes the lives of individuals.[13]

Paul acknowledged that Gentiles were formerly outsiders, but he went on to confirm they had become fellow citizens. The first Gentile believers admitted into a church composed of Jewish Christians may have rightly felt uncomfortable in this community with a Jewish worldview and Jewish practices. They may have been wondering about their status. Were they there on probation or as visitors like the God-fearing Gentiles who attended synagogues? Was their position like that of resident aliens in a Greek city or like that of noncitizens in Rome? Perhaps stories filtered back to them about how Peter and other Jewish Christians abandoned the practice of table fellowship with Gentile Christians at Antioch (Gal. 2:11-14). But Paul wanted them to feel at home. He stuck up for the Gentiles in Antioch and remained uncompromising in his welcome to Gentiles. Gentile Christians were not adherents or visitors or second-rate citizens in the believing community; they were full members.[14]

If the community is viewed as a house or household, Gentile believers are not household servants but sons and daughters with all the rights of inheritance. The Father to whom they have access is the same Father as that of Jewish brothers and sisters. It is by the same Spirit that his Gentile and Jewish children alike acknowledge him as their Father.[15]

Not only are Jews and Gentiles members of God's family, they have been made into a place of worship, a new temple. The old divisive temple of Jerusalem was replaced by a community built on the foundation of apostles and prophets. Christ is the chief cornerstone that locks all things together, growing this new people into "a holy temple" and dwelling place for God. This is the gospel's potential; the vision of Ephesians 1:22-23 would be realized. God would place all things under Christ's feet as the head of the Church.[16]

APPLICATION

Today, the abolition of the barrier separating Jews and Gentiles may not be as revolutionary as it was for Paul and his associates, but there are other dividing differences within the human family which are equally irrelevant in the sight of God and ought to be irrelevant in the sight of his children.[17] Paul knew how serious his fellow Jews took the barrier that separated Jews from Gentiles in the temple. He was falsely accused of violating this rule, and it led to his arrest and detainment in Roman custody. While the Jew-Gentile divide isn't a concern today, there are many barriers and "dividing walls" in American society. Racial, gender, religious, social, economic, and educational barriers threaten the Church today. Paul proclaims a radical vision in which Christ's new creation dismantles old social structures with their prejudices, hostilities, and tensions that divide the Church. Through the cross, Christ put to death the hostility that comes with bigotry (Eph. 2:16). Martin Luther King Jr. once mourned that the most segregated hour of the week was the church hour on Sunday. As Capes, Reeves, and Richards write in *Rediscovering Paul*: "According to Paul, anyone who maintains and promotes such division denies the ultimacy of the cross and the lordship of Jesus through whom all barriers have been overthrown. Bigots are enemies of the cross."[18]

Believers don't have to settle for this state of affairs in their churches and communities. Thankfully, Christians are not left alone. Christ has accomplished unity on behalf of all believers on the cross and has endued them with the power of his presence, the Holy Spirit.

The second half of Ephesians is filled with practical instructions for how to live. Paul tells his readers to get rid of the vices that characterize their pre-Christian lives and to put on the virtues of Jesus. He warns them to quit such practices as lying, stealing, sexual immorality, coarse language, excessive anger, bitterness, greed, and many others. He affirms that behavior change is not only possible, it is part of their divine calling and God's purpose for them (Eph. 1:4; 2:10; 4:1).[19] To this list of unchristian behavior and attitudes is added prejudice and racial animosity. Paul had already encouraged them that it was possible to form one new humanity. That call for unity is appropriate for the Church today. If the Church Paul presents in Ephesians 2 stands for overcoming the fundamental division of humanity into Jew or Gentile, it stands also for overcoming all divisions caused by tradition, class, color, nation, or groups of nations.[20]

This is no doubt an ideal not yet fully realized, but the insistence of this letter is that the ideal will one day be seen as a worldwide reality thanks to the completeness of Christ's reconciling sacrifice.[21] When Scripture gives a glimpse of the end, there is racial, ethnic, and cultural unity in the new creation. There may be a temptation to ask: If Christians now compose a "new" or "third race," then should all racial and cultural distinctions be abolished? The beautiful picture in Revelation is one of racial, ethnic, and cultural distinctives on display in the new creation. Therefore, let all believers be encouraged to celebrate all kinds of diversity in the Church. Churches are (or should be) filled with people of diverse origins, pasts, privileges, hopes, despairs, and perhaps even suspicions of those not like them. Now these people are enabled by the work and rule of Christ to contribute in common repentance and common faith their various peculiarities, histories, experiences, and gifts to the peaceful common life of God's people.[22]

DISCUSSION QUESTIONS

1. Can you identify the racial, gender, religious, social, economic and/or educational barriers in your community that may threaten the mission of the Church today?
2. Are there attitudes and practices in your church that keep you separated from the community you are commissioned to reach? Can you think of barriers Christians erect to keep us separate?
3. Unity of God's diverse people is a key theme of Ephesians 2. What are some things your church is doing to pursue unity in your community?
4. Can you think of ways that the unity of God's diverse people could send a message to the world

that God's plan is being accomplished in Christ Jesus?

5. Ephesians may have been written to Gentile believers who were dismissive of the church's Jewish roots. Have you reflected on the Jewish nature of the foundation of the early church? Have you seen anti-Semitism show up in your interactions with fellow believers?

6. How could it be helpful to see Christianity as a "new race" united in Christ to carry out God's mission?

in 2 Corinthians 5:16-21. A form of the word "reconciliation" occurs five times in this passage. To reconcile, in its simplest form, denotes "the action by which peace is made between two personal enemies." Reconciliation is the work of a mediator whose role is to "make hostility cease" and "to lead to peace."[2] This peace is not merely the absence of strife but a change from anger, animosity, or hostility to love, friendship, or intimacy. The essential change here is not in one's feelings but a change of relationship in the social or political realm.[3] Paul says that God initiated this work of reconciliation through the work of Jesus, and God gave Paul and his fellow apostles (and ultimately all disciples) the ministry of reconciliation.

This passage begins with Paul saying that, from the moment believers access Christ's saving work, they "regard no one from a worldly point of view," even though Paul confesses on the believer's behalf that they once regarded Christ in this way (2 Cor. 5:16). To regard someone from a "worldly" point of view refers to applying standards based merely on human, external values — be it status, ethnicity, wealth, talent, or appearances.[4] In Paul's pre-conversion days, he judged Christ using those standards and came to the wrong conclusion. Prior to his conversion, like many of his fellow Jews, Paul would have dismissed claims that Jesus was the Messiah because he would have regarded it as unthinkable that God's Messiah could be crucified like a criminal.[5]

Since God vindicated Jesus by raising him from the dead after his crucifixion, no one has the right to look at Christ from that worldly viewpoint. God's grace received through faith is the only way a person's eyes might be opened to the glory of Christ and who he is. At that point, when eyes are opened and one becomes a believer, that person's status has changed in a major way.

The most common understanding of 2 Corinthians 5:17 is that if one places one's faith in Christ, they are a new creation. Several of the most popular translations portray the sense that something dramatic happens to the individual who becomes a Christian. The NASB states that if anyone is in Christ, "he is a new creature." The ESV, CSB, and NKJV all say that if anyone is in Christ, "he is a new creation" (the ESV has the footnote: "new creature"). This is a true statement. But the force of this verse is even more dramatic.

The NRSV states "there is a new creation" and the NIV states, "if anyone is in Christ, the new creation has come." If translated literally from the original language, the phrase reads, "if anyone in Christ – new creation." I think the NRSV and the NIV come closest to capturing the full impact of this verse. Paul is saying that when someone believes the gospel, another part of new creation bursts in upon the world. New creation began when Jesus rose from the dead. By God's Spirit, it happens again every time somebody becomes a Christian and will go on happening until the new creation is complete.[6] As true and as important as it is to realize that, as individuals, Christians are "new creatures/creations," one shouldn't reduce the original phrase to just that. In this context, Paul is not describing the personal dimension of a new birth. Rather, he is announcing the dramatic recovery of the world, formerly alienated and dislocated but now placed under the rule of Christ.[7]

Paul states, "The old has gone, the new is here!" On the individual level, this is true. The believer can now leave his/her former life of sin behind and live a new life empowered by the Holy Spirit in pursuit of Christlikeness. At the same time, Paul is saying something about new creation breaking in on the scene, and as it grows, the elements of the present creation, groaning for redemption, are being overcome. This is pointing to the end of the book of Revelation to the one who says, "I am making everything new!" (Rev. 21:5).

Many Christians think the ultimate goal is to escape this present world and go to a better one, somewhere totally different (like a disembodied state in heaven). There will be an intermediate state for those who die in Christ. Their souls will exist in Christ's presence in heaven, but that is not the final destination. The New Testament's vision of our final destination is a recreated heavens and earth where the Father and Son rule over us in a personal, physically present way. This newness is being anticipated, already breaking into the world when people are joined to Christ in faith and live by faith in Christ.[8] Believers are to be both signs of the expected new creation and workers in that cause. This is one of the reasons the Church mattered to Paul. Christian communities are signposts of the glory of the new creation.[9] As seen in chapter one, all ethnic and cultural diversity will be maintained in the new creation as God's united people worship in the presence of Jesus (Rev. 21:26). This is where Christ's redemption program is heading.

The idea of the redemption of creation is important in the discussion of the reconciliation of all people in Christ. In light of the reconciliation God has offered in Christ, he has given believers the ministry of reconciliation (2 Cor. 5:18-21). In this portion of the passage, there are three key assertions:

1. God is the driving force behind the redemption of humanity. Reconciliation comes solely at God's initiative.
2. God acted through Christ's death, and Christ alone is the means of reconciliation.
3. God continues to act through those who have been

reconciled. They have the privilege and
responsibility to share in this great act of love and
are to call others to be reconciled to God.[10]

As seen earlier, the definition of reconciliation is more than
just a change in feelings or attitudes. Reconciliation is not
simply a cessation of hostilities or an uneasy truce. It refers to
the mending of broken relationships. That healing comes from
God making people right through faith and changing them
from enemies to friends.[11]

On one level, this is related to followers of Jesus
announcing the saving work of Jesus and calling others to a
lifestyle of discipleship. In light of new creation, believers are
to not only announce this message of reconciliation, but they
are to model reconciliation in a community context. For Jesus,
being reconciled to a fellow human being was more important
than offering sacrifices at the altar (Matt. 5:24). The gospel is
lived when Christians practice reconciliation among
themselves and exemplify it before their neighbors.
"Ambassadors of reconciliation" (2 Cor. 5:19) have the
opportunity to promote peacemaking in communities full of
factions, distrust, and mutual suspicions.[12]

Paul's ministry doesn't just proclaim reconciliation; it is the
content of his ministry. The ministry of reconciliation involves
more than simply explaining to others what God has done in
Christ (as important as that is). It requires that one become
active in reconciling work. Paul's own work as a reconciler is
clear in both of his letters to the Corinthians.

In 1 Corinthians, Paul tries to put an end to divisions in
the church that manifested around a few of their favorite
teachers: "I follow Paul... I follow Apollos... I follow
Cephas... I follow Christ" (1 Cor. 1:12). He intervenes to

prevent members of the church from bringing lawsuits against each other in pagan courts (1 Cor. 6:1-11). He cautions those with no convictions against eating meat sacrificed to idols lest they become a stumbling block to those with a "weak conscience" in this matter (1 Cor. 8:1-13). He rebukes the entire congregation for celebrating the Lord's Supper in a manner that left the poor humiliated and hungry (1 Cor. 11:17-34).

In 2 Corinthians, he insists they forgive the repentant offender (2 Cor. 2:5-11), and the entire letter seeks to bring reconciliation between himself and the church.[13] Elsewhere, Paul encourages the Philippian church to help Euodia and Syntyche reconcile (Phil. 4:2-3). Paul's letter to Philemon was sent with the hope that he might see reconciliation between Philemon and Onesimus. Throughout his letters, Paul displays hope that Jews and Gentiles will see themselves as a united community in Christ (Eph. 2:16; Gal. 3:28).

Paul modeled this behavior with the hope that his churches would imitate him. His desire was to form new communities that would cut across normal boundaries and barriers, practice obedience to the Lord, and model a new way of being human and a new kind of power. The Church was to be a community acting as signposts pointing toward the new creation. They were to be a prototype of what was to come. That is why unity and holiness mattered to Paul. These new creation communities were to function like beacons in a dark place.

The Church is a place of reconciliation between God and the world, a place where humans might be reconciled to one another as a signal of what God intends to do for the whole of creation.[14] The Church should model an integration and reconciliation that challenges the social and cultural divisions in the world outside.[15]

APPLICATION

This points to the task of the Church and its importance in the discussion of various forms of ethnic and cultural reconciliation. Humans may attempt to reconcile with each other, but if they are not also reconciled to God, no real reconciliation is possible. Reconciliation obliges Christians to reorder their lives around God. A believer's changed orientation, when they no longer live for themselves, spills over into all their relationships. Continuing to harbor animosity toward others contradicts any claim to be reconciled to God. As Paul mentioned in 2 Corinthians 5:12, Christians no longer evaluate others using worldly criteria. They must look at others from God's vantage point. This spurs them on to do the work of reconciliation because they have been reconciled to God.[16]

Paul believed God was establishing his presence by the Holy Spirit in all the world and that it was his call to bring into being, through preaching the gospel, communities where that would be a reality. But since that reality is all about reconciliation — between God and creation, God and humanity, and humans with one another — the large-scale universal vision cannot help but be birthed and grow to affect human tensions in churches and between individuals.[17]

It is not enough to bring men and women to a right understanding of the proper doctrines (even though that is important). Paul is not only interested in an abstract doctrine of reconciliation but in the concrete task of reconciliation. The Church is called by God to be a reconciling force. That means it must adopt the status of a servant, and it must be active in a ministry of healing in individual communities, including the act of bringing hostile factions together in Christ.[18]

As ministers of reconciliation, where broken things are seen, Christians should be about the work of healing and repair. Reconciliation has been realized in Christ; the Church should then act like it. Believers should be changed by and proclaim to the world this reality: that God has provided the means by which humanity can be rightly related to him and to each other.

DISCUSSION QUESTIONS

1. Have you ever been advised to ignore issues like racial reconciliation and been told to "just preach the gospel"? Can you see any connection between gospel preaching and racial reconciliation? Is pursuing reconciliation a "distraction" from more important things like evangelism?

2. Reconciliation has been defined as the work of a mediator whose role "is to make hostility cease" and "to lead to peace." Does the Church have a role in this within your community? How are you and/or your church working to make hostility cease in your community?

3. Reconciliation is not simply a "cessation of hostilities or an uneasy truce." How should our churches be active in pursuing reconciliation?

4. Should we only pursue reconciliation between God and humans? Is there room for believers to pursue reconciliation between people groups? Why or why not?

5. This chapter gave several examples of how Paul pursued a variety of types of reconciliation:

personal, corporate, ethnic, etc. In what ways does your church pursue any of a variety of types of reconciliation?

CHAPTER SIX

THE CHRIST HYMN AND RECONCILIATION

W hat is the source of the racial tension seen in some communities? One could go back several centuries and look at the roots of this tension and inequality (not only the causes rooted in slavery but also tension that comes with immigration and refugee settlement). That discussion needs to have historians and sociologists involved to get at the heart of those problems. Regardless, the Church should be a source of hope for these problems, leading the way in working toward the healing of all these wounds. At times, Christians fail to act because they don't know where to start. At other times, they fail to act because of fear. They are afraid that working toward true equality in their communities will cost them something. An African American pastor friend recently posted this on social media: "Everyone loves equality until they realize it means they might have to give something up." Reconciliation carries a significant cost.

Some Christians subconsciously don't want to give up their privilege, materials, or advantage. Part of the problem is that many Christians don't see the prosperity of their brothers and sisters as connected to their own prosperity or the prosperity of their communities. The Church needs to catch a vision of their communities flourishing and act toward that end.

This vision leads to an exegesis of Philippians 2:5-11. The posture of Jesus displayed in this passage should be the posture all Christians are willing to take in this work for racial harmony. The humility of the incarnation is a cue to believers as to what they should be willing to give up for the sake of harmony and unity. Jesus emptied himself of the privilege of equality with God in order to give himself up on behalf of humanity. Paul exhorts that this attitude should be the attitude of all believers.

THE CHRIST HYMN — PHILIPPIANS 2:6-11

Philippians 2:6-11 is the prime example of an early Christian hymn, known as the "Christ Hymn." It is thought to be a pre-formed piece Paul used in this letter to teach this church about Jesus' pre-existence, the form of his incarnation, and the nature of his exaltation. With verses 6-11, Paul launches into a narrative about Christ that becomes one of the most exalted, most beloved, and most discussed and debated passages in Paul's letters.[1]

The influence of the letter to the Philippians on the Church at large seems disproportionate to its length, largely due to this passage. This hymn elegantly sums up Paul's teaching about the person of Jesus Christ and the nature of God while providing a magnificent description of Jesus Christ: pre-existent, equal with God, God incarnate, fully human, a servant, totally obedient to the Father, exalted by God to the highest place in heaven or on earth, and the object of worship for all created beings to the glory of God the Father.[2]

Even though this passage contains such great doctrinal

teaching about the person and nature of Jesus, the primary purpose of including this hymn in the letter was not theological or Christological but ethical. The goal he had in mind was to not only give instruction in doctrine but to reinforce instruction in Christian living. He did this by using Christ as the ultimate model for moral action, as the supreme example of unselfish conduct.[3]

What was going on in this church to prompt Paul to include this passage in his letter? Although Paul doesn't spell it out explicitly, there appears to be some sort of division or conflict in this church. This conflict appears to be internal and external. Before the transition in this letter at the beginning of chapter two, Paul had been calling the Philippians to conduct themselves in a manner worthy of the gospel.

The unity of the church would be a sign of destruction to those who opposed them. This opposition had caused suffering, but Paul wanted to impress upon the Philippians that the unity within the church would lead to the church fulfilling God's good purpose for them.

Paul starts chapter two by looking backward immediately at what he has just written, the exhortation to live as "citizens worthy of the gospel" by "standing firm in one Spirit against the opposition." Then, Paul begins by asking the Philippians a series of rhetorical questions (all of which assume a "yes" answer):

- IF – you have encouragement from being united in Christ (and you have);
- IF – you have any comfort from his love (and you have);
- IF – you have shared in the Holy Spirit (and you have);

- IF – you have found compassion and sympathy (and you have);
- THEN – make my joy complete by being united.

What is the basis for their unity? It is Christ and the Holy Spirit and the encouragement, comfort, and compassion found in them. How will believers accomplish this unity? By considering others better than themselves and by putting the interests of others first. If any Christian community is to live in harmony, it must no longer look out for its own interests to the exclusion of others.[4]

When believers properly evaluate themselves in light of the holiness of God, the gospel, and the example of Christ, they are compelled to set the interests of others above their own. Problems of disunity end when respect for others is discovered. This is what Paul commands us to do: consider others better than ourselves. Naturally, no one thinks this way. But the divine command directed to the Christian community implies divine assistance to achieve the impossible.[5]

Paul is not seeking uniformity of opinion. Instead, he asks that church members strive for deep affection for one another; that they develop a common desire to live in harmony by renouncing factions, empty conceit, and self-interest; and that they adopt a humble attitude that considers others better than themselves. In such a climate, unity thrives, the Church grows, and the individual Christian (and the cause of the Church worldwide) is strengthened in the faith.[6]

THE ETHIC OF THE CHRIST HYMN

Many have looked at Philippians 2:6-11 as the place where Christology began.[7] It has been mined for its testimony to early Christian worship and hymnody. But in verse 5, Paul prepares the way for this deeply theological and Christological section by presenting it as ethical instruction.

The comforting note about this call to self-denial is that Christ has already done it. If Christians think they are being called to egregious acts of self-abasement, they should be encouraged and inspired that Christ has given up far more than they could ever imagine.

As Paul moves into this theologically ripe passage, he begins by describing Christ Jesus as "being in very nature (or in the form of) God." Paul believed Jesus was equal to God the Father. The term for "nature" or "form" in Greek is *morphe*. The term *morphe* denotes the genuine nature of something (or someone). By saying that Jesus had the form or nature of God, it may be understood that Jesus possessed "the essential nature and character of God."[8] Paul is saying that Christ is God.[9]

Even though Jesus was equal to God, sharing his nature, he "did not consider equality with God something to be used for his own advantage." A more literal translation of this phrase carries the sense of "snatching" or "grasping" for equality with God. This phrase refers more to an attitude, not an act, a direction of mind one has toward something already in one's possession.

Here it means that Christ's attitude was not to regard his equality with God as something to take advantage of or something to be used for his own benefit. Jesus did not see his equality with God as something that allowed him to snatch, grab, or acquire things for himself. To the contrary: "Jesus saw God-likeness essentially as giving and spending oneself out."[10]

N. T. Wright has expressed that the "real theological emphasis of the hymn… is not simply a new view of Jesus. It is a new understanding of God."[11] The identity of God is grounded as much in self-abasement and service as it is in exaltation and rule. The God who is high can also be low, because God is God not in seeking his own advantage but in self-giving.[12]

This passage could be paraphrased, "Christ Jesus, who, *because* he was in the form of God, did not regard his equality with God as something to be used for his own advantage, but to be used for the advantage of others. Hence, he emptied himself…".[13] Jesus did not understand his equality with God as a matter of being served by others, but as something he could express in service, obedience, self-renunciation, and self-humiliation for others.

Jesus emptied himself, or "made himself nothing." What Jesus gave up in coming to earth was immense. From a position of "equality with God," which entailed the immediate presence of the Father and the Holy Spirit as well as the continuous praise of the angels, he came to earth where he had none of these. The magnitude of what he gave up is beyond humanity's power even to imagine, for none of us has seen what heaven is like. Scripture paints the picture that believers will be overwhelmed by the splendor of what Jesus left behind when he became man.[14]

And what did Jesus submit to here on earth? He took the form of a servant. He was born into a very common family in the very obscure, little town of Bethlehem. And even more striking, he was born in the very humble setting of a stable and laid in a manger. He lived in relative obscurity, and even though at times he drew large crowds, he was left with very few real followers. He died a death that symbolized to his people a curse, and the Romans executed him as a common rebel.

In the incarnation, the pre-existent Christ entered the stream of human life as a person without advantage, claiming no rights or privileges of his own, for the express purpose of placing himself completely at the service of all people.[15] So, Jesus exchanged the honor and glory of divine status in the heavenly palace, where myriads of angels served him, for the form of a servant and the dishonor, the loss of all status, that death on a cross entailed.

As a result of Jesus' faithful obedience, God raised him to the highest place (literally, he "super-exalted" him) and gave Jesus the name above every name. The name Jesus was given is Lord (*kurios*). This name should be equated with Yahweh's holy name. Paul looks into the future and sees a day of universal acclamation of all heavenly and earthly creatures (and even those beneath the earth). When the name that belongs to Jesus is expressed, "every knee [will] bow... every tongue [will] acknowledge that Jesus Christ is Lord" (Phil. 2:10-11).

Here Paul alludes to Isaiah 45:23. This passage describes the worship of Yahweh. Paul took scriptural language regarding worship of Israel's one God and applied it to the risen Jesus. It was in Jesus' humility (in his act of emptying himself of his privilege) that he was expressing and enacting his equality with God, and therefore, it qualified him to exercise the unique, divine sovereignty over all things.

His exaltation to the highest position is not a matter of gaining or regaining equality with God. He never lost that. This is how he accessed the sovereignty of God.[16] Paul points to a passage (Isa. 45:23) that describes the Servant of the Lord. It is through the suffering, humiliation, death, and exaltation of the Servant that the sovereignty of the one true God comes to be acknowledged by all nations.[17]

Christ's exaltation should not be seen as a reward for his humility but as the natural result of it. Philippians 2:8 could be paraphrased as, "Because Jesus made himself nothing..." (the narrative continues in verse 9) "... therefore God exalted him." This provides evidence as to how God's kingdom works: in the divine order of things, self-humbling leads to exaltation. This is how God has designed the universe.[18]

APPLICATION

What a wonderful hymn and concise theology lesson. For Paul, however, application was the whole reason behind this passage (because good theology should always lead to proper behavior). The Christ Hymn presents Jesus as the supreme example of the humble, self-sacrificing, self-denying servant whom Paul urged the Philippians to model in their relations toward one another.

Paul's motive is not only to give instruction in doctrine but to reinforce instruction in Christian living. He does this by appealing to the conduct of Christ. The hymn, therefore, presents Christ as the ultimate model for moral action. While this hymn may have been composed to teach its hearers and readers something about Jesus' pre-existence, incarnation, and exaltation, part of Paul's motive in including it is ethical. He wants his hearers to change their way of living based on this knowledge.

For the Philippians, this was a call to unity motivated by the humility of Christ for our benefit. Now Paul is calling the Philippians to humble themselves for others and be unified.

Moving forward to today, this returns us to the reason we started an examination of this important passage. How do Christians apply the truths of the Christ Hymn to the issue of racial reconciliation in the Church in the 21st century? Let's use the example of Christ's incarnation as a model for churches and Christian organizations in regard to improving relations between the races and to encourage more diverse networks in terms of members, churches, and leaders.

Jesus gave up tremendous comfort to serve humanity. What are Christians willing to give up to help their brothers and sisters flourish?

When home, car, or electronic repairs are needed, what is

the one question no one enjoys asking? I'd say it's, "What is this going to cost me?" The Church needs repair. So, the same question needs to be asked. At the very least, there needs to be the acknowledgement that certain segments of American communities are better taken care of than others.

The American church should be able to acknowledge that, on the whole, white Westerners often enjoy certain privileges and benefits not shared by all, such as more positive interactions with those in authority and more representation in popular culture. If those privileged believers could see the amount of influence and affluence they have in comparison to some less fortunate brothers and sisters in Christ, it should prompt them to act. Even if they personally don't see the influence and affluence, perhaps they can at least acknowledge they possess freedom from certain concerns or fears many minorities face every day. If Jesus was willing to leave the comfort and glory of heaven, there is no amount of sacrifice too great for today's believer.

The natural inclination of all humans is to serve themselves. The root of idolatry is selfishness. Humanity has always pursued and attempted to grasp at equality with God. People want to be the ones in charge, to have — or at least be perceived as having — ultimate power, freedom, and control of their destinies (and by extension, the destiny of others). Everyone wants to set the standards of purity, righteousness, and goodness for others.

If Christians in North America would listen better to their brothers and sisters in Christ from minority communities, they might see that the privileged hold advantages that give them a false sense of superiority. Subconsciously, these advantaged believers may think, "We've got it all together, thus there must be something inherently better about us and our way." Many in the majority culture fall into the passive category of benefiting from advantages, and they want to hold on to that. This is the heart of injustice. The "passive" state of advantage loves the comfort of stability and consistency. Believers in this category may have difficulty admitting that this continues to benefit them.

What is the Church to do? It begins by acknowledging there is a lack of equality in society. The next step is asking this question, individually: "How am I complicit in this current state of inequality?" Most Christians may not be using their freedom for the purposes of exploitation, but passivity ignores the reality of injustice and inequalities in life experiences, life opportunities, and social relationships for many people of color.

Christians need to recapture the vision of the kingdom of God and the vision of how this kingdom project ends. The apostle John received a picture of the worship of Jesus in heaven, and he saw a great multitude from "every nation, tribe, people and language" crying out, "Salvation belongs to our God, who sits on the throne, and to the Lamb" (Rev. 7:9-10).

If the Church can become captivated by this vision in heaven, then she can work toward it now here on earth. This will not be easy, and it bears a cost, but the vision John sees is so beautiful that it is worth working toward. Believers have to see how the flourishing of all brothers and sisters contributes to the flourishing of each individual because every believer is part of the same family.

If Christians are ever going to see a just, flourishing society, they need to follow the example of Jesus in the incarnation: crossing boundaries, purposely laying down privilege (the thing to be grasped), and dying.

Brian Key, Preaching Pastor and Residency Director at Redeemer Fellowship, Kansas City, has been a tremendous resource in helping me walk through these issues. He sees three points of reference in the Christ Hymn and the pursuit of racial reconciliation:

Crossing Boundaries: Christ crosses two boundaries. He leaves the comfort and glory of heaven, and he moves from pre-existence to finite human being. He does this for the benefit of others. He does this to affect the peace and unity for which all people long but no human effort can attain.

One lesson to learn is that the one with the power has to be the one to cross the bridge and help those without power. Where should those with the advantages go in order to work for reconciliation? Those with the power and influence should be initiating efforts to bring about reconciliation and flourishment. This is more than pulpit exchanges and dialogue. It is moving into less fortunate areas and setting up shop, pitching tents, and utilizing influence to help others succeed. There needs to be partnerships in ways that puts the majority culture under minority leadership.

Leveraging Advantages for the Good of Others: This may be the most uncomfortable thing Christians in the majority culture will deal with, but it is essential to the concept of Christians loving their neighbors. In order to lay down advantages, one is required to identify those advantages. However, these can be difficult to acknowledge. They just seem like normal life. The individualistic culture allows for individuals to think only about themselves. Laying down privilege involves beginning to "look not only to your own interests but also the interests of others" (Phil. 2:4).

Dying: Once the vision of the beautiful, flourishing kingdom of God is seen, are privileged Christians willing to die to what has benefitted them? Does the Church believe that the identity God offers is beautiful enough and safe enough to lay down advantages for the benefit of others?

God's bountiful provision of every spiritual blessing (Eph. 1:3) and everything needed for life and godliness (2 Peter 1) is available to every believer. Does the Church believe this is enough to be able to die to "selfish ambition and vain conceit?" Are individual Christians willing to consider others as greater than themselves (Phil. 2:3)? And if believers aren't willing to die to those privileges, is it possible that they have not fully appreciated or appropriated the self-sacrifice of Jesus?

FINAL THOUGHTS ON THE CHRIST HYMN

The heart of the Christ Hymn is the story of someone of great power and prominence leaving his position of privilege to work for the thriving of others. While Christ left his position of privilege, he did not give up the privilege itself. Instead, he leveraged it.

He was the only possible sacrifice to enable the welcome of sinners into the presence of a holy God. He used his power to do for humanity what they didn't have the power to do for themselves. He spent his unlimited resources and riches of grace on humanity to welcome them, not just as participants in the realities of his kingdom but as coheirs. He offered a seat at the table and a share in the inheritance.

This is going to be hard work. It is going to call for sacrifice: sacrifice of position, influence, power, money, and pride. But these things are nothing compared with what Christ gave up in the incarnation and as he followed through with his obedience and death on the cross.

This is going to take time and effort, but the call to unity given to the Philippians extends to the Church today. The example Paul gave for this difficult and demanding work was the example of Christ, who did not use his position of privilege for his own advantage but gave it all up for the possibility of unity and reconciliation.

This understanding of Philippians 2:5-11 provokes a series of questions:

- What would the Church look like to the world if believers could get this right?
- What impact would this have for the gospel?
- What might happen if Christians were humble enough to admit that some people have advantages over others on the basis of race?
- Beyond that, what if those Christians who possess this advantage choose not to use it for themselves?
- What if the Church learned from the example set out by Christ in the Christ Hymn and chose to lay aside privilege and influence for the betterment of others?

The work of true racial reconciliation is hard work. It is going to cost something. What are the comforts Christians need to be willing to give up for the benefit of others? Is it enough to confess that some people in society have advantages not available to others, acknowledging inequality?

No, there must be more.

Believers must sacrifice for the betterment of those who are not flourishing. As citizens of the kingdom of God, how do Christians see themselves in relation to those less fortunate? And what are they willing to give up in order to help others flourish? What is this going to cost? How do believers leverage privilege for the good of others?

Christ gave himself completely, and in doing so, he renounced the benefits of his privilege. Oftentimes, Christians chase after access to power and status instead of spending themselves on behalf of the hungry and oppressed. Instead of clamoring for worldly power, access, and influence, believers should see that true power is in self-humiliation. What a powerful example the Church could show the nation if she worked hard to make the vision of the kingdom come to fruition on earth as it is in heaven.

THE MINISTRY OF RECONCILIATION

The New Testament makes a compelling case for the Church to live as a community that transcends racial and ethnic differences. If churches in the U.S. would live out the reality of this vision, it would have a powerful effect in American society. And likewise, if the Church fails to live out this reality, it compromises the truth of the gospel. For churches and institutions to continue to put up with racial inequality and injustice that springs from a lack of racial reconciliation is a disturbing sign of unfaithfulness to the message and power of the gospel.[19] The Church has the task of embodying "the ministry of reconciliation" in the world. In other words, the Church is called to expand and extend the same vocation that was Israel's: to bring God's salvation "to the ends of the earth" (Isa. 49:6). Over twenty years ago, Duke Divinity professor Richard Hays called racism heresy and stated that one of the Church's most urgent pragmatic tasks was to form communities that seek reconciliation across ethnic and racial lines.[20] This is no less true today than when he wrote it in 1996.

The Church has an incredible opportunity to declare to the world the power of the gospel in the unification of humanity, but they can only seize that opportunity in the midst of sacrifice as they strive to reflect the diversity seen in the new creation.

DISCUSSION QUESTIONS

1. If your church were to compose a mission statement inspired by Philippians 2:5-11, what would be some of the major action items?

2. List all of the ways Christ denied himself in this passage (Phil. 2:5-11). Now, reflect on the phrase, "In your relationships with one another, have the same mindset as Christ Jesus…"

3. What can be learned from the idea that "it is through the suffering, humiliation, death and exaltation" of Jesus that the sovereignty of God comes to be acknowledged by all nations (Isa. 45:23)?

4. Jesus gave up tremendous comfort to serve humanity. Can you think of what you and your church may be willing to give up to help others flourish?

5. When observing inequality in the world, how did Jesus respond? How should the Church follow his example?

6. How could you and/or your church initiate reconciliation efforts in your community?

APPENDIX

ACTION ITEMS

1. THE ROADMAP TO RECONCILIATION

Dr. Brenda Salter McNeil, a leader in the pursuit of reconciliation, lays out a four-step plan for reconciliation in her book, *The Roadmap to Reconciliation*:[1]

1. Realization: understanding a new reality. The need for change is acknowledged, and individuals become aware of their ethnic identities. The severity of social problems comes to light. Even the privileged see change is in the best interests of everyone. Resources are used to serve and interact with people in need.
2. Identification: your people become my people. Individuals embrace the stories of others and build empathy. Outsiders are seen and heard in new ways.
3. Preparation: getting ready for lasting change. This takes place after the hard work of being present

and available, of listening and learning, of building trust and establishing credibility. Individuals then need to decide to do things significantly different from how they've done them before. This may involve shifting operational paradigms, making structural changes, and implementing policy changes within organizations.

4. Activation: actively working for reconciliation. This is where individuals activate the skills and competencies learned in the preparation phase by actively getting involved. The privileged need to advocate for change.

The heart of this project stems from the idea Salter McNeil stresses in her book:

> We must never think that we are finished once we have spoken up, be it on Facebook or in the boardroom. Talking isn't enough. We need to expand the bandwidth of our conversations by influencing decisions within political, economic, and social systems and institutions.[2]

2. HOLISTIC CHANGES

The pursuit of racial reconciliation extends beyond just whites and African Americans. The Church also needs to listen to Latin, African, Asian, and Native American voices. Duke Kwon is pastor of Grace Meridian Hill Church in Washington, D.C. His three-step process for working toward racial reconciliation is based on the offices of Christ — prophet, priest, and king.[3]

It begins with the least impact and lowest social cost and moves on to greater impact and cost. The first step is in "The

Prophetic Dimension." The Church needs to publicly repudiate past sins which have fostered inequality. Christians need to correct errors in their beliefs and practices. The foundations of cross-cultural discipleship need to be taught. The Church needs to provide a vision for culturally equitable and inclusive institutions.

The second dimension in which work needs to be done is in "The Priestly Dimension." Here, Christians need to lead in personal and corporate repentance. The Church needs to listen and weep with those who weep. Believers need to foster relationships across differences and hostilities. A culture of truth-telling should be cultivated.

The third dimension in which work needs to be done is "The Kingly Dimension." Christians need to lead in the administering of institutional change toward racial equality. They need to undo racist and exclusive policies and procedures while rebuilding leadership structures around power-sharing and inclusion. And the Church needs to exercise institutional authority in the face of opposition.

3. ORGANIZATIONAL CHANGES

What does working toward unity look like for institutions like state conventions and local churches? Are there any administrative steps? Mark Croston Sr., national director of Black Church Partnerships for LifeWay Christian Resources, provides practical action items for working toward racial reconciliation.[4] I've listed some of them here:

1. Overcome fear. Repercussions are expected from those who either fear the loss of privilege or who don't want to admit it is real in the first place.
2. Hire diverse leaders. Business leaders know if they

want to reach a diverse community, that community needs to see ethnic representation in their company's leadership. Entities must hire more qualified leadership from among the ranks of people of color and must put more people of color in positions of leadership and influence if they want to work toward racial reconciliation.

3. Work hard to be partners not patriarchs. Patriarchs make decisions and inform the minority constituents. Partners get to sit at the table, cook the food, and lead in the dinner table discussions.

4. Persevere. As has been stated all along, this is not going to be easy. Many know this from trying to manage change in their own churches and organizations. When they try to implement concepts like forgiveness and repentance for privilege, it won't go over well in many cases. The natural, fallen disposition is to grasp at and hold onto advantage, not use it for the benefit of others. Some leaders may pay an incredible price, but if this is the right thing (and it is), it is worth it.

5. Love. The Great Commandment that calls Christians to love their neighbor as themselves must be elevated. The call to see brothers and sisters of color as neighbors deserving of love has to be taken seriously. These are people who deserve the Church's work to see them flourish.

EXAMPLES OF THOSE AT WORK

Here are some examples of churches and organizations that are working toward the goal of diversity and reconciliation. They are at different levels of participation, but hopefully these examples encourage others to take the next step toward unity.

Frontline Church, Oklahoma City

Frontline Church in Oklahoma City launched with fifty people from Josh and Nancy Kouri's home in 2005 and has grown to include four congregations with around twenty-six hundred in weekly attendance. Frontline's leadership examined the racial make-up of the church, and it was at around 90 percent white. They were convicted, finding the numbers unsatisfactory. They wanted their membership to more fully reflect the diversity of the communities in which their congregations met. Their teaching and preaching focused on the gospel with an eye on the sin patterns within the church that may have led to such segregation. They saw that racial division is a gospel issue, and they confronted it on their preaching platforms.

Not being satisfied with only preaching on racism and diversity, they took intentional steps to resolve this issue. They gathered minority leaders and just listened to them and their stories. They asked these leaders about their experience shepherding minority churches in a majority culture. What were the difficulties and challenges they faced? They also asked how they could help. On the basis of these listening sessions, Frontline planned changes based on what they learned.

Frontline also hosted a symposium on the gospel and race in Oklahoma City. They invited leaders from their city to hear from practitioners leading their churches and organizations in diversity and inclusion. The goal was to encourage pastors in the area to work through the question of how to lead their churches in light of God's desire for unity among ethnic groups.

This has led Frontline to reflect on its own leadership. As members examined themselves, they realized they only had two non-white elders from their total of twenty-one. This led them to work on an initiative to raise up minority leaders from within their own ranks. The goal of this initiative was to see more minority leaders in churches around their city and state, not just in their own church.

North Phoenix Baptist Church

At one time, North Phoenix Baptist Church was one of the largest Southern Baptist churches in the West with over twenty-three thousand members. When Noe Garcia was called as senior pastor in 2016, the average attendance was less than one thousand. In a metropolitan area that is over one-third non-white, North Phoenix Church was over 90 percent white in active membership. The only minorities on staff were Garcia and one of the custodians. The only time attendees saw people of color on the platform was during a music special with a gospel singer or a spoken word performer.

Garcia intentionally began to make changes. He preached on racism and reconciliation. He also wanted the church to see that the gospel can break racial barriers. They needed more than to simply hear a preacher say it. He ensured that people of color were on the stage for more than just the "ethnic" stuff. Garcia said, "If the congregation only saw white faces on the platform, they may wonder if there was any place for them at the church. Is there any potential for leadership for us?" He wanted the church to reflect the diversity of the community, so he made sure the people on the platform reflected that diversity. He also reshaped the staff, hiring quality staff members while keeping diversity in mind.

For Garcia, reconciliation worked both ways. He

confronted friends and colleagues of color who had cultivated prejudiced views toward whites because of their past experiences with racism. Garcia counseled those colleagues, saying they could not allow those experiences to infect their thinking and actions. Garcia even worked to make sure North Phoenix Church didn't go too far the other way by making diversity an idol. When one of their satellite campuses began to compile a staff of primarily one (non-white) ethnicity, he called them out and made sure they pursued diversity as well.

Garcia's efforts have not come without difficulty. He lost regular members who were put off by the discussion on race and inclusion. Some left because they felt threatened by a shift in the balance of authority away from the dominant culture. As the worship services began to reflect diversity in style and in leaders, some people left because it wasn't their preference. Beyond losing members due to these changes, Garcia also received threats against himself and his family.

In spite of the difficulty of the work to pursue reconciliation and inclusion, North Phoenix Baptist Church's attendance has more than tripled, and its weekly attendance much more reflects the demographics of the Phoenix metropolitan area than before Garcia's arrival.

Redeemer Fellowship, Kansas City

Redeemer Fellowship in the Westport neighborhood of Kansas City began as a church replant of First Calvary Baptist Church in 2008. Church members started with a desire to bring about transformation "in [them]selves, in [their] neighborhood, and throughout [their] city."[5]

After a few years, the elders of the church had a conversation about where they were as a church in regard to race and reconciliation. The church was located in the middle of a racially divided city. Members had every intention of sowing the gospel in this community and seeing God draw all types of people to himself, but they didn't see that happening in their church. They were a fast-growing congregation, but eight years after relaunch, they were still predominantly a white church.

Brian Key was then Pastor of Gospel Communities at Redeemer. He confessed that he felt like he was not always comfortable being himself as an African American at the church. He acknowledged that he often preached differently and worshiped differently when he went back home to preach and worship in black churches. He was not comfortable totally expressing himself at Redeemer. If Key, who was a part of the church from the start, felt that way, then that must also have described many of the minority members and attendees. They must have felt like they needed to yield to the majority culture in the church.

The leaders of the church made a conscious decision to do something about that. Key's role changed from small-groups pastor to preaching pastor. They wanted Key to preach more frequently at their two campuses (Midtown K.C. and Johnson County, Kansas). This was a sacrifice of the lead communicators. They had to give up a large portion of their time on the platform to make this work. Key now preached twenty to twenty-five times a year across the two campuses. Key was not encouraged to shape his style to match the other preaching pastors, but was asked to preach in a manner that expressed his heart, a heart shaped by his black church upbringing.

Key was also asked to form a worship band that reflected the style of black worship experience. The other worship bands tried to learn those songs as well so their congregation would see that this was a culture shift that involved everyone, not just a feature of special "gospel music" Sundays. They developed a more diverse song catalog that exemplified the diversity they desired in the church.

All these changes were made to send a message to their congregation and especially to the people of color who attended. When a church has minorities in volunteer roles but not in leadership, that tells minority attendees there is a ceiling preventing people like them from becoming leaders in the church. However, when a black pastor is preaching the gospel, leading worship, and leading through eldership, it says something to the visitors and attendees. Perhaps they could become leaders here, too. Perhaps they could utilize their gifts to their fullest capacities.

Redeemer Fellowship committed resources to make these changes happen. In addition to being a preaching pastor, Key became the director of their minority pastor residency. These residents were full-time staff members with the opportunity to pursue a theological education at Midwestern Baptist Theological Seminary, finishing with master's degrees by the end of the residency. The residents were exposed to the ministry process of Redeemer. They sat in elder meetings and other pastoral meetings. They learned all the aspects of church ministry and experience. They also worked on ministry plans to implement in the areas for which they were responsible. By the end of their two-year residency, the goal was for these residents to plant a church, join a church-planting team, or join the staff of an established church.

This residency had two facets. Not only did the leaders of Redeemer train and shape minority leaders, but they allowed these minority pastors to shape the culture of Redeemer and teach the church about their experience. The leadership of Redeemer prepared the church for this shift by showing how diversity and racial reconciliation springs from the heart of

God. The pursuit of diversity and inclusion and the sermons against racism were not imposed on the church from some outside sociological viewpoint or movement. It was based in the Scriptures. As Key says:

> If you have a beef with me [about this discussion], you have a beef with Jesus! God has planned for a reconciliation of diverse people groups from before the foundation of the world, has made it possible in human history through the person and work of Jesus, and will bring that work to completion in Jesus at the end of time. We long to do all that we can to see that reality expressed to bear witness to the plan, purchase, and promise of God in our context.[6]

The Southern Baptists of Texas Convention

Richard Taylor provides some perspective from a denominational position. Taylor serves as the point person for the "Look Like Heaven Initiative" for the Southern Baptists of Texas Convention. At the time of this publication, Taylor encourages pastors in his network to lead their churches in cross-cultural interchanges and intentional relationships across ethnic and cultural lines as a lifestyle. Some first steps of this initiative include: pulpit, praise team, or choir swap; joint revivals and worship services; coffee or breakfast with other pastors; and joint mission trips and service projects.

Taylor is a member of a multi-ethnic church and is currently serving as interim pastor of another multi-ethnic church in a highly diverse community. Both churches understand the need to make sure the staff, leadership, and worship style reflect the diversity of the community.

Taylor was asked, "What can churches in predominantly white communities do to be more aware of the issues that face people of color?" He responded that the key to this, on both an institutional and personal level, is for churches with a desire to become more diverse to begin building relationships with people that are different from their dominant culture. While it must be intentional, it cannot be forced. This approach holds a delicate tension. There has to be a genuine desire to want to know people and learn about the issues, concerns, hurts, and celebrations of another culture. Church members must be willing to be students rather than teachers, which is counter-cultural because predominantly white communities and congregations assume that their role is to change or fix problems before fully understanding the needs of the communities. Prayer walking, prayer driving, or just praying help sensitize the heart.

Taylor also gave advice for what pastors and leaders can do when racial issues reach a flashpoint and dominate a news cycle. Many times, when issues arise in nearby communities, if there are no relationships with people in that community, predominantly white congregations are usually silent or adopt a biased view shaped from the greater political and social narrative rather than factual information. Taylor's recommendation was to suspend judgments and opinions until all the facts are clear. However, when there are clear signs of injustice and systemic inequalities, he suggested not to sit in silence but to stand for what is right. Taylor cited Reverend Dr. Martin Luther King Jr.:

> Cowardice asks the question — is it safe? Vanity asks the question — is it popular? Expediency asks the question — is it political? But conscience asks the question — is it right? There comes a time when one must take a position that is neither safe, popular, or political; but because it is right.[7]

When asked what resources he recommended for white pastors to educate themselves on the need for diversity or reconciliation, Taylor replied that "the absolute greatest thing that a white pastor can do is genuinely build relationships with other pastors and people who do not look, think, or even vote like they do. Sit down as a student or missiologist and learn. Have hard conversations without taking on a defensive posture."

This is a missional issue. The Church can display the ministry of reconciliation to the world, but believers must ask hard questions to get there. How are Christians displaying this reconciliation with the people they worship with, break bread with, and share lives with? If they aren't displaying this, what is the reason? Is it because the Church is too comfortable with the way things are now? Are believers afraid? Is it because certain Christians can't get past their biases against other people groups? The Church needs to be willing to spend the effort to work through this and find out why many Christians aren't displaying the ministry of reconciliation in this way.

NOTES

INTRODUCTION

1. Staff Report, "Ferguson as It Unfolded," *St. Louis Post-Dispatch*, https://www.stltoday.com/news/special-reports/michael-brown/. Accessed March 12, 2019.
2. Emma Vandelinder, "Racial Climate at MU: A Timeline of Incidents This Fall," *Columbia Missourian*, November 6, 2015, https://www.columbiamissourian.com/news/higher_education/racial-climate-at-mu-a-timeline-of-incidents-this-fall/article_0c96f986-84c6-11e5-a38f-2bd0aab0bf74.html. Accessed March 12, 2019.
3. Jarvis Williams, "Biblical Steps toward Removing the Stain of Racism from the Southern Baptist Convention," in *Removing the Stain of Racism in the Southern Baptist Convention*, eds. Jarvis Williams and

Kevin Jones (Nahsville: B&H Academic, 2017), 26-27.

4. Williams, 27-28.

CHAPTER ONE: BEGIN WITH THE END IN MIND

1. Stephen Gandel, "The 7 Habits of Highly Effective People (1989) by Stephen R. Covey," The 25 Most Influential Business Management Books, TIME. August 9, 2011, http://content.time.com/time/specials/packages/article/0,28804,2086680_2086683_2087685,00.html. Accessed July 17, 2018.

2. Franklin Covey, "Habit 2: Begin with the End in Mind," Franklin Covey: The Ultimate Competitive Advantage. Accessed February 15, 2019, https://www.franklincovey.com/the-7-habits/habit-2.html.

3. Covey, "Habit 2."

4. Tim Chester, *From Creation to New Creation* (London: Paternoster, 2003), 89.

5. George Beasley-Murray, "Revelation, Book of," in *Dictionary of the Later New Testament & Its Development*, eds. Ralph Martin and Peter Davids (Downers Grove, IL: InterVarsity Press, 1997), 1034.

6. Beasley-Murray, "Revelation, Book of," 1034-1035.

7. David Aune, *Revelation 1-5*, Word Biblical Commentary (Dallas, TX: Word Books, 1997), 362.

8. Craig Keener, *The NIV Application Commentary: Revelation* (Grand Rapids, MI: Zondervan, 2000), 188-189.

9. Robert Mounce, *The Book of Revelation*, New

International Commentary of the New Testament
(Grand Rapids: Eerdmans, 1977), 148.

10. Keener, 189.
11. Keener, 191-192.
12. Keener, 195.
13. Leon Morris, *Revelation*, Tyndale New Testament
    Commentary (Downers Grove: InterVarsity Press
    Academic, 1987), 113-114.
14. Keener, 243.
15. Keener, 247.
16. Keener, 250.
17. John Newport, *The Lion and the Lamb* (Nashville,
    TN: Broadman Press, 1986), 321.
18. Carl Ellis, "The Sovereignty of God and Ethnic-
    Based Suffering," Desiring God, October 6, 2005,
    https://www.desiringgod.org/messages/the-
    sovereignty-of-god-and-ethnic-based-suffering.
19. J. Richard Middleton, *A New Heaven and a New
    Earth: Reclaiming Biblical Eschatology* (Grand Rapids:
    Baker Books, 2014), 173-174.
20. Keener, 246.
21. Middleton, 281-282.

CHAPTER TWO: AS IT WAS IN THE BEGINNING

1. Michael Bird, *Evangelical Theology* (Grand Rapids:
   Zondervan, 2013), 660.
2. See also Proverbs 31:8-9 as well, words from a
   mother to her son, King Lemuel.
3. This will be discussed more fully in chapter five.
4. Brenda Salter McNeil, *Roadmap to Reconciliation*
   (Downers Grove: IVP Books, 2015), 23-24.

5. Smithsonian National Museum of Natural History, "Modern Human Diversity – Skin Color," http:// humanorigins.si.edu/evidence/genetics/human-skin-color-variation/modern-human-diversity-skin-color. Accessed March 13, 2019.

6. Salter McNeil, 24.

7. Gordon Wenham, *Genesis 1-15*, Word Biblical Commentary (Dallas: Word Publishing, 1987), 215.

8. Daniel Block, "Table of Nations" in *International Standard Bible Encyclopedia*, Volume 4, ed. Geoffrey Bromiley (Grand Rapids: Wm. B. Eerdmans, 1988), 712.

9. Victor Hamilton, *The Book of Genesis, Chapters 1-17*, New International Commentary on the Old Testament (Grand Rapids: Wm. B. Eerdmans, 1990), 346.

10. Salter McNeil, 25-26.

11. Hamilton, 347.

12. See Christopher Wright, *The Mission of God's People* (Grand Rapids: Zondervan, 2010), 66-70.

13. Wright, 71.

14. Wright. 71.

15. See Romans 1:1-6; 9:24-29; 16:25-27; Ephesians 3:1-6.

16. Tim Chester, *From Creation to New Creation* (London: Paternoster, 2003), 137.

17. Chester, 139.

18. Chester, 146.

19. Chester, 140.

20. Wright, 71.

21. J. Richard Middleton, *A New Heaven and a New Earth: Reclaiming Biblical Eschatology* (Grand Rapids: Baker Books, 2014), 379.

22. F. F. Bruce, *The Epistles to the Colossians, to Philemon and to the Ephesians*, New International Commentary of the New Testament (Grand Rapids: Wm. B. Eerdmans, 1984), 57-58.
23. Millard Erickson, *Christian Theology* (Grand Rapids: Baker Book House, 1985), 514-515.
24. Bird, 660.
25. Ralph Smith, *Old Testament Theology* (Nashville: Broadman & Holman, 1993), 245.
26. Donald Guthrie, *New Testament Theology* (Downers Grove: InterVarsity Press, 1981), 952.
27. John Walton, *The NIV Application Commentary: Genesis* (Grand Rapids: Zondervan, 2001), 138-139.

CHAPTER THREE: THE DIVERSITY OF THE EARLY CHURCH AND CONFLICT RESOLUTION

1. Richard Longenecker, *The Expositor's Bible Commentary: Acts* (Grand Rapids: Zondervan, 1995), 3.
2. Joel B. Green, "Acts of the Apostles," in *Dictionary of the Later New Testament & Its Development*, 7-8.
3. Green, "Acts of the Apostles," 14-15.
4. This is a summary of 2 Kings 17.
5. H. G. M. Williamson, "Samaritans," in *Dictionary of Jesus and the Gospels*, eds. Joel Green and Scot McKnight (Downers Grove: InterVarsity Press, 1992), 726-7. See Josephus, Antiquities 18, 29-30.
6. Mishnah Shebiith 8:10.
7. Sirach 50:25-26. (Sirach is also known as Ecclesiasticus in some editions of the Apocrypha).

8. Scot McKnight, "Gentiles, Gentile Mission," in *Dictionary of the Later New Testament*, 389.

9. McKnight, "Gentiles," 389. See also Alan Segal, *Rebecca's Children: Judaism and Christianity in the Roman World* (Cambridge, MA: Harvard University Press, 1986), 177.

10. Chad Chambers, "Gentiles," in *Lexham Bible Dictionary*, ed. John Barry (Bellingham, WA: Lexham Press, 2016). See also Terrance Donaldson, *Paul and the Gentiles: Remapping the Apostle's Convictional World* (Minneapolis: Fortress, 1997), 51-74. See also the ancient Jewish religious work Jubilees 15:26.

11. McKnight, "Gentiles," in *Dictionary of Jesus and the Gospels*, 260.

12. Dennis Durst, "The Nations," in *Lexham Bible Dictionary*.

13. See Lev. 20:24-26; Ezra 10:11 for examples. See also non-canonical Jewish literature like *The Epistle of Aristeas*, 139-42 and Philo's *On the Life of Moses*, 1:278.

14. James D. G. Dunn, *Beginning from Jerusalem* (Grand Rapids: Eerdmans, 2009), 395.

15. McKnight, "Gentiles," 259.

16. McKnight, "Gentiles," 259.

17. David Williams, *Acts*, New International Biblical Commentary (Peabody, MA: Hendrickson, 1990), 39.

18. Andrew Lincoln, "Pentecost," in *Dictionary of the Later New Testament*, 906. There is a tradition that Moses received the Law fifty days after Passover.

19. Joachim Jeremias proposes there may have been over one-hundred thousand pilgrims in Jerusalem

for the festivals, *Jerusalem in the Time of Jesus* (Minneapolis: Fortress Press), 1969, 83.

20. Dunn, 158-159.
21. Eckhard Schnabel, *Acts*, Exegetical Commentary on the New Testament (Grand Rapids: Zondervan, 2012), 118
22. John Polhill, *Acts*, New American Commentary (Nashville: Broadman & Holman, 1992), 102.
23. Schnabel, 119.
24. Polhill, 106.
25. Robert Wall, "Acts of the Apostles," in *The New Interpreter's Bible*, Vol. X (Nashville: Abington Press, 2002), 110.
26. Darrell Bock, *Acts*, Baker Exegetical Commentary of the New Testament (Grand Rapids: Baker Academic, 2007), 256.
27. Bock, 257.
28. Wall, "Acts of the Apostles," 111. See Acts 11:1-18; 14:27-15:29; 21:17-26.
29. Bock, 257.
30. Wall, "Acts of the Apostles," 111.
31. Walter Bauer and Frederick Danker, *A Greek–English Lexicon of the New Testament and Other Early Christian Literature* (*BDAG*) (Chicago: University of Chicago Press, 2002), 319.
32. Bauer and Danker, 269-270.
33. Polhill, 179.
34. Dunn, 248.
35. Polhill, 180; see also Jeremias, 131-133.
36. Dunn, 251.
37. Dunn, 252-253.
38. Bock, 258.
39. Wall, 114.

40. Polhill, 180.
41. Polhill, 181.
42. F. F. Bruce, *The Book of Acts*, New International Commentary on the New Testament (Grand Rapids: Eerdmans, 1988), 130.
43. Bock, 262.
44. Bock, 259.
45. Bock, 261.
46. Dunn, 248.
47. Dunn, 253-254.
48. Bruce, *The Book of Acts*, 131.
49. Dunn, 257.
50. Wall, 135.
51. Polhill, 214-215. Stephen's defense before the Sanhedrin in chapter 7 was cast in language to show that God had been interacting with his people outside of the traditional boundaries of Israel.
52. The use of the term *edei* implies that God was behind the necessity for Jesus to go through Samaria.
53. Wall, 137.
54. Bock, 331-332.
55. Polhill, 218.
56. Polhill, 223. See also Henry Cadbury, *The Book of Acts in History* (Eugene, OR: Wipf & Stock, 1955), 17.
57. Bock, 33.
58. Bock, 339. Cf. Ben Witherington, *The Acts of the Apostles* (Grand Rapids: Eerdmans, 1998), 296.
59. Wall, 143.
60. Polhill, 226.
61. Polhill, 228. See also Erich Dinkler, "Philippus und

der Anēr Ainthiops," in *Jesus und Paulus* (Göttingen: Vandenhoeck & Ruprecht, 1957), 85-95.

62. Bock, 347.
63. Wall, 135.
64. Polhill, 249.
65. Polhill, 252.
66. Dunn, 392-393. See Daniel 1:8-16; 1 Maccabees. 1:62-63.
67. Dunn, 393.
68. Mishnah 'Ohalot 18.7; Bock, 392.
69. Dunn, 395.
70. Dunn, 395-396.
71. Dunn, 396.
72. Dunn, 397-398.
73. Bock, 397.
74. Dunn, 400.
75. Wall, 167.
76. Bock, 401.
77. Bock, 404.
78. Bock, 410.
79. Bock, 410.

CHAPTER FOUR: DESTROYING THE DIVIDING WALL OF HOSTILITY

1. Josephus, *Wars of the Jews,* 5.193-194.
2. Mark Allan Powell, *Introducing the New Testament* (Grand Rapids: Baker Academic, 2009), 325.
3. Powell, 334.
4. Markus Barth, *Ephesians: Translation and Commentary on Chapters 1-3*, Anchor Bible, Vol. 34 (New York: Doubleday, 1974), 10-12.

5. Andrew Lincoln, *Ephesians*, Word Biblical Commentary (Dallas: Word Publishing, 1990), 132.

6. F. F. Bruce, *Colossians, Philemon, Ephesians*, NICNT, 292.

7. *The Epistle of Aristeas*, 139-142.

8. Lincoln, *Ephesians*, 141.

9. See Tacitus, *Histories*, 5.1-13.

10. Powell, 335.

11. Lincoln, *Ephesians*, 143-144.

12. Bruce, *Colossians, Philemon, Ephesians*, 295-296; see also *Epistle to Diognetus*, 1; Clement of Alexandria, *The Stromata*, 6.5.41.6.

13. Bruce, *Colossians, Philemon, Ephesians*, 278.

14. Bruce, *Colossians, Philemon, Ephesians*, 302.

15. Bruce, *Colossians, Philemon, Ephesians*, 303.

16. Dunn, 1113.

17. Bruce, *Colossians, Philemon, Ephesians*, 301.

18. David Capes, Rodney Reeves and Randolph Richards, *Rediscovering Paul* (Downers Grove: IVP Academic, 2007), 231.

19. C. E. Arnold, "Ephesians, Letter to," in *Dictionary of Paul and His Letters*, eds. Gerald Hawthorne and Ralph Martin (Downers Grove: InterVarsity Press, 1993), 247.

20. Lincoln, *Ephesians*, 161-162.

21. Bruce, *Colossians, Philemon, Ephesians*, 330.

22. Barth, 311.

CHAPTER FIVE: THE MINISTRY OF RECONCILIATION

1. D. A. Horton, "Many Ethnicities," Right Now Media, https://www.rightnowmedia.org/

Training/Post/Preview/185592. Accessed
February 2019.

2. Ralph Martin, *2 Corinthians*, Word Biblical
Commentary (Dallas: Word Publishing, 1986), 146.
3. Joseph Fitzmyer, *To Advance the Gospel* (Grand
Rapids: Wm. B. Eerdmans, 1998), 164-165.
4. Moyer Hubbard, *2 Corinthians*, Teach the Text
Commentaries (Grand Rapids: Baker Books,
2017), 109.
5. Colin Kruse, *2 Corinthians* (Downers Grove:
InterVarsity Press, 2015), 168.
6. N. T. Wright, *Reflecting the Glory* (Minneapolis:
Augsburg Press, 1998), 50-51.
7. Martin, 146.
8. Wright, *Reflecting the Glory*, 51.
9. Wright, *Paul and the Faithfulness of God* (Minneapolis:
Fortress Press, 2013), 1489.
10. David Garland, *2 Corinthians*, New American
Commentary (Nashville: Broadman & Holman,
1999), 288-289.
11. Garland, 290.
12. Bird, 559.
13. Garland, 292.
14. Wright, *Paul and the Faithfulness of God*, 1491-1492.
15. Wright, *Paul and the Faithfulness of God*, 1511.
16. Garland, 299.
17. Wright, *Paul and the Faithfulness of God*, 1515.
18. Garland, 300.

CHAPTER SIX: THE CHRIST HYMN AND RECONCILIATION

1. Gordon Fee, *Paul's Letter to the Philippians* (Grand Rapids: Wm. B. Eerdmans, 1995), 192.
2. Gerald Hawthorne, "Philippians, Letter to the," in *Dictionary of Paul and His Letters*, eds. Gerald Hawthorne and Ralph Martin (Downers Grove, IL: InterVarsity Press, 1993), 712.
3. Hawthorne, *Word Biblical Themes: Philippians* (Waco, TX: Word Books, 1987), 66-67.
4. Hawthorne, *Philippians*, Word Biblical Commentary, vol. 43 (Dallas, TX: Word Incorporated, 1991), 69.
5. Hawthorne, *Philippians*, 70.
6. Hawthorne, *Philippians*, 71.
7. Michael Gorman, *Inhabiting the Cruciform God* (Grand Rapids: Wm. B. Eerdmans, 2009), 75-76.
8. Gorman, 9. See Ralph Martin and Brian Dodd, eds., *Where Christology Began: Essays on Philippians 2* (Louisville: Westminster John Knox, 1998).
9. Hawthorne, *Themes*, 67.
10. Hawthorne, 68.
11. Hawthorne, 70. Hawthorne cites C. F. D. Moule, "The Manhood of Jesus in the New Testament," in *Christ, Faith and History*, S. W. Sykes and J. P. Clayton, eds. (Cambridge: Cambridge University Press, 1976), 97.
12. N. T. Wright, *The Climax of the Covenant* (Minneapolis: Fortress Press, 1993), 84.
13. Richard Bauckham, *Jesus and the God of Israel* (Grand Rapids: Eerdmans, 2008), 45.

14. Wright, *Paul and the Faithfulness of God*, 1491-1492.
15. Gorman, 70.
16. Millard Erickson, *Christian Theology* (Grand Rapids: Baker Book House, 1985), 770.
17. Gorman, 71. Cf. Mark 10:45.
18. Bauckham, 44.
19. Richard Hays, *The Moral Vision of the New Testament* (New York: Harper Collins, 1996), 441.
20. Hays, 441.

APPENDIX

1. I've briefly summarized chapters 4-7 of her book, *Roadmap to Reconciliation*.
2. Salter McNeil, *Roadmap to Reconciliation*, 99.
3. This material was taken from material that Kwon presented and was posted on twitter by a listener, https://twitter.com/KathrynAnnette/status/913239792510529537. Accessed September 28, 2018.
4. I've briefly summarized Mark Croton Sr.'s essay, "Administrative Steps Toward Removing the Stain of Racism from the Southern Baptist Convention," in *Removing the Stain of Racism*, 81-103.
5. "Our First Sunday." Redeemer Fellowship Kansas City, https://redeemerkansascity.org/our-story-1. Accessed November 5, 2018.
6. Brian Key. Interview by Bill Victor, November 5, 2018.
7. This is from Martin Luther King's speech: "A Proper Sense of Priorities," delivered February 6, 1968, Washington, D.C.

ABOUT THE AUTHOR

Bill Victor serves in the Developing Leaders Group and as Scholar in Residence for the Missouri Baptist Convention. He earned his Ph.D. in New Testament from Southwestern Baptist Theological Seminary. He has taught as an adjunct professor at Southwest Baptist University, College of the Ozarks, Hannibal LaGrange University, and Liberty University's School of Divinity.

He has served several churches as interim pastor and has authored another book, *Scenes of the Kingdom*. He and his wife Chris have a daughter.

Made in the
USA
Middletown, DE